I was up late last night reading ***Debt of Love***. It is truly inspiring and filled with so much grace. I couldn't stop the tears. Holy Tsar-Martyr Nicholas II and his precious Holy Family are with us. Alleluia!

— Jonathan Jackson
Emmy Award-winning American Actor

[We] would like to thank Ariane Trifunovic Montemuro for writing this wonderful book and for showing us all the light of God's love which shines eternal upon the memory of this very special Holy Martyr and his blessed family.

— Their Royal Highnesses Prince Vladimir and Princess Brigitta Karadjordjević
Excerpt from their Preface

April 4, 2019
To: Ariane Trifunovic Montemuro

Dear Handmaiden of our Lord Jesus Christ,
Well done good and faithful servant of our Lord.

I Rejoice in the Lord for all you have done to bring further prayer to the Royal Martyrs Tsar Nicholas and Family, not only prayer but presenting us with truthful accounts of the Passion Bearers, and those who loved them from the beginning to the end up until their great holy Glorification and thereafter their hundredth anniversary of their holy martyrdom.

What an honorable account and then again what a blessing for others to share in their spiritual beauty and love for one another as well as Russia that has found that we ask God for forgiveness and renewal of our love for God to great spiritual heights.

The photos are outstanding: some I had never seen before, and the iconography as well shines in this book that one will want to venerate them as they open up the pages.

The contributors to your book including your family have also brought this book to be honored and respected.

In the end the greater blessing is the Tsar-Martyr Nicholas II scholarship fund for Holy Trinity Seminary, Jordanville, New York as these students will find comfort knowing they are being blessed by the Tsar-Martyr, and can study onward in their preparation for the Holy Priesthood by his prayers.

I cannot wait to have this book in my hands, and I cannot wait to share it with others, especially those who will now understand we truly have been told lies and so much propaganda that in the end God always reveals Himself to others who love Him, and His Church Holy Orthodoxy! Truly our Lord has revealed to us the holy Royal Martyrs Tsar Nicholas II and family.

You helped in this regards.

Our Lord God has written these words with you!

Thanks to your beloved husband Anthony who has helped you move this book forward.

Keep up the good work for our Lord and those who love Him!

Peace to your soul!

Humbly in our Lord Jesus Christ,
+Father Nektarios Serfes
Who always prays for you and family!

The "bleeding" icon of the Holy Royal Martyrs.
The myrrh that streamed from it was the color of blood.

Troparion — Tone 5

Meekly didst thou endure the loss of thine earthly kingdom, the bonds and multifarious sufferings, bearing witness unto Christ even to death at the hands of the godless, O great passion-bearer, divinely crowned Emperor Nicholas. Wherefore, Christ God hath crowned thee in the heavens with a martyr's crown, together with thine empress, thy children and thy servants. Him do thou beseech, that He have mercy on the Russian land and save our souls.

Kontakion — Tone 3

Thou wast shown to be an imitator of the intercessor of Myra in Lycia, O right faithful Tsar; for, fulfilling the Gospel of Christ, thou didst lay down thy life for thy people, and didst spare the guilty, even those guilty of murder. For these things thou hast been sanctified by the blood of martyrdom, as a great martyr of the Church of Christ.

***Both of these translations are taken from the Service celebrated on the 4/17 of July in "Commemoration of the Holy Imperial Martyrs of Russia: Emperor Nicholas, Empress Alexandra & their children, Alexis, Olga, Tatiana, Matia & Anastasia slain by the godless", which is found in the July (Vol. XI) Menaion of the Orthodox Church published by the St John of Kronsdadt Press, Liberty, Tennessee, copyrighted 2011. The translations are the work of the good & faithful servant of God, the late Reader Isaac (tonsured into the lesser schema as Monk Joseph just before his repose on January 27, 2017) Lambertson.*

Tsar-Martyr Nicholas II and his family of Holy Royal Martyrs were devoted to the people of Serbia. If they lived today, they would no doubt wholeheartedly support the rebuilding of desecrated Serbian Orthodox churches and monasteries in Serbia's holy land, Kosovo-Mehotija.

"Weep for Kosovo" by Ariane Trifunovic Montemuro
www.thedecanifund.org

Preface

THEIR ROYAL HIGHNESSES
PRINCE VLADIMIR AND PRINCESS BRIGITTA
KARADJORDJEVIĆ

Holy Royal Martyrs, pray for us.

Their Royal Highnesses
Prince Vladimir and Princess Brigitta
Karadjordjević
Of Serbia and Yugoslavia

HRH Prince Vladimir is the eldest son of the late HRH Prince Andrej and the grandson of HRH King Aleksandar I Karadjordjević of Serbia and Yugoslavia. HRH Prince Vladimir is also the great-great-great-great grandson of Her Majesty Queen Victoria, Queen of the United Kingdom of Great Britain and Ireland and Empress of India, and a nephew of Her Majesty Queen Elizabeth, Queen of the United Kingdom and Other Commonwealth Realms.

Serbian Royals Share Their Love for Tsar-Martyr Nicholas II of Russia

If one mentions "Russia" within Serbia one experiences a wonderful feeling of warmth and kinship that, in my humble opinion, may not exist in this magnitude between any other Orthodox nations. If one were to merely whisper the name of the Holy Martyr Tsar Nikolai II into the ear of any patriotic Serb, one would see the tears well up in that Serbs eyes. The Serbian pain of losing such a national treasure, as was the Imperial family of Russia, could only be greater in Mother Russia itself. Such is the love and respect for Holy Martyr Tsar Nikolai II and his family within Serbia.

It has been said that Russia and Serbia are not two peoples living in two separate states, but rather two subdivisions of one people. Everything brings us towards this definition — our same precious Orthodox Christianity, our almost similar culture and language, our same political positions, our alliances in all past conflicts, even the "world" ones, our same geopolitical and geostrategic interests. And as something that forges the ties between these previously mentioned things — an intensive emotional relation and love between Russians and Serbs throughout the entire history. If we explain the relation between Russians and Serbs by this definition, everything becomes very clear and simple. And all rhetorical and demagogic maneuvers opposite to it collapse in a blink of the eye.

The love for Tsar Nikolai II which is felt by the present members of the Yugoslav royal family began many years ago, when King Aleksandar I of Yugoslavia was enrolled at the famous Page Corps in St. Petersburg. Tsar Nikolai II had given Aleksandar, along with his brother, Djordje, and his father, King Petar I, refuge in Russia. Aleksandar was often invited to the Winter Palace where he would share time with members of the Russian Imperial family. King Aleksandar never forgot the love and Christian brotherhood that he was to have shared with Tsar Nikolai II and the other members of the Imperial family.

A number of historians over the past century have tried to malign Tsar Nikolai and the Imperial Family of Russia but this historical incorrectness has always fallen on deaf ears within Serbia because it is the Serbs who very well remember the love and Christian brotherhood which the Tsar also harboured for our people and our country and he showed it through his absolute support for Serbia, both before and during the First World War, right up to the day that mother Russia was robbed of her blessed Imperial Family.

The Serbs have never forgotten that during the utter misery of World War I, when the Serbian army was forced to retreat through Albania under attack from the Austrian and German armies, that the Tsar sent a letter to Russia's allies (France and Great Britain), warning that Russia would withdraw from the war if they did not send ships to help the Serbian army. This act alone saved so many Serbian lives.

It was wonderful to see the unveiling of a great statue of the Holy Martyr Tsar Nikolai II in Belgrade in 2014. It is yet another reminder of the love and absolute respect that the Serbian people share for this great man, his family, and for Russia and the Russian Orthodox church.

Prince Vladimir and I would like to thank Ariane Trifunovic Montemuro for writing this wonderful book and for showing us all the light of God's love which shines eternal upon the memory of this very special Holy Martyr and his blessed family.

HRH Princess Brigitta Karadjordjević
HRH Prince Vladimir Karadjordjević

Their Royal Highnesses
Prince Vladimir and Princess Brigitta Karadjordjević
standing in front of the monument to
Tsar-Martyr Nicholas II of Russia located on
Kralyna Milana Street in the heart of Belgrade, Serbia.
In 2014, Russian Orthodox Patriarch Kirill blessed this
monument of the Tsar, saying "The memory of Russian Tsar
Nicholas II was kept alive by the Serbian nation even as it was
forbidden in the Russian nation to say his name aloud."

Debt of Love

Ariane Trifunovic Montemuro

Preface by Their Royal Highnesses
Prince Vladimir and Princess Brigitta Karadjordjević

Foreword by Archimandrite Nektarios Serfes

Afterword by Jonathan and Elisa Jackson

Ideas into Books: Westview®
Kingston Springs, Tennessee

Printed with the blessing of

His Grace

Bishop L O N G I N

\+ + +

Ideas into Books®
WESTVIEW
P.O. Box 605
Kingston Springs, TN 37082
www.publishedbywestview.com

ISBN 978-1-62880-163-7

First edition, September 2019

Unless otherwise noted, all scripture passages are from the King James Version of the Bible.

Please note that original spellings have been maintained from all source materials.

Cover Design by
Ariane Trifunovic Montemuro.
The cross on the cover was a gift from Elisa Vultaggio Jackson.
Photograph of cross and cover layout by
Jennifer Wright at Chromatics, Nashville, TN.
Graphic Design by
Elaine P. Millen, Teknolink Marketing Services, Charlotte, NC.

The author thanks the Holy Trinity Icon Studio for permission to use this image: http://iconstudio.jordanville.org/st-royal-family-1/

Printed in the United States of America on acid free paper.

Serbian Bishop Longin blesses Ariane's book. His Grace is pleased that donations inspired by her book will be given in honor of Tsar-Martyr Nicholas II. These donations will help the Orthodox Faith grow by supporting the needs of Holy Trinity Seminary, in Jordanville, New York.

You can support the Orthodox faith that Tsar-Martyr Nicholas II loved by sending your donation directly to: Holy Trinity Seminary, P.O. Box 36, 1407 Robinson Road, Jordanville, NY 13361. In the memo section of your check please write: "In honor of Tsar-Martyr Nicholas II," or donate online at www.hts.edu/support.html.

His Grace, Bishop Luke of Syracuse
Rector of Holy Trinity Seminary and
Abbot of Holy Trinity Monastery
Jordanville, NY.

Letter to the Reader of this Book

From His Grace, the Rt. Rev. Luke
Bishop of Syracuse, Abbot of Holy Trinity Monastery and
Rector of Holy Trinity Seminary,
Jordanville, NY.

In these days of growing mistrust in authorities and in and governments, it is important for people to understand why this is.

We know from the Scriptures that all authority is from God. In a Christian monarchy, it is understood that God Himself anointed the ruler, who then held this high calling as his sacred trust, and dedicated his life to the welfare of his people, regardless of his own personal tastes. This was not only the social contract between ruler and those whom he ruled, but a recognition of the source of all good, God Himself.

Tsar Nicholas, II of Russia was such a ruler. Like all humans, he had his faults and his frailties, but he deeply felt and believed in his holy duty to the peoples he ruled in the Russian Empire. He built more churches than any other ruler; ever. He also supported many monastic houses. He spent his personal funds on institutions to help the underprivileged. He sponsored the renewal of traditional Orthodox holy art and music.

Ultimately, he gave the final sacrifice. He suffered martyrdom, along with his venerable family, refusing to leave his country in its time of troubles. His death was not just an execution, but the mindful elimination of "the hand that held back" the forces of evil. Even people who did not value him were shocked by his death, the death of "the anointed one."

Evidently, God allowed this, as the Russian people no longer understood the need to have a tsar. Even so, they obtained an intercessor before the throne of God. Those who feel something missing in our present times of anarchy, endless conflicts, and lack of moral direction, can now turn to the Right-believing Royal Passion-bearers as beacons of hope, and as examples to emulate. This was an august family united by Christian love. Tsar-Martyr Nicholas, II gave up his earthly throne to obtain his place in the heavenly kingdom.

If those who read this book are inspired by the story of this remarkable family of saintly martyrs, please realize that the Romanov family had among their highest priorities to support the important institutions of the Holy Orthodox Church such as monasteries, seminaries and parishes. The Russian Orthodox Church Outside of Russia in general, and monastics and seminarians at Holy Trinity Monastery and Seminary in Jordanville, NY in particular, have had a profound veneration of the Royal family dating back many decades, beginning at a time when many of our fathers and students here were from families of the white Russian emigration. The Royal Martyrs were glorified by the Russian Orthodox Church Outside of Russia all the way back in 1981, a full nineteen years before they were glorified by the Church in Russia.

The traditional, patristically-grounded seminary formation of young men who are preparing to dedicate their lives to serve well the Holy Orthodox Church and its faithful is as important in our day as it has ever been. Funding academic scholarships is a very important part of our mission, and this is exactly the type of effort that the Tsar-Martyr and his family would have personally supported.

+ + +

Donations to Holy Trinity Seminary in Jordanville, N.Y. can be sent to:

Holy Trinity Seminary
P.O. Box 36
1407 Robinson Road
Jordanville, NY 13361

Please specify that the donation is being made in honor of Tsar-Martyr Nicholas II.

Holy Trinity Orthodox Seminary is an institution of higher learning under the jurisdiction of the Russian Orthodox Church Outside Russia. The mission of Holy Trinity Orthodox Seminary is to serve the Russian Orthodox Church Outside Russia by preparing students for service to the Church as clergy, monastics, choir directors, cantors, iconographers, and lay leaders. To learn more about Holy Trinity Orthodox Seminary, log onto their website: www.hts.edu.

A Message Regarding Donations

I sincerely hope and pray that Ariane's heartfelt book, *DEBT OF LOVE*, inspires her readers to honor Tsar-Martyr Nicholas II and his family by supporting our beloved Holy Trinity Seminary, Jordanville, New York, in his name.

The Romanov dynasty always had a profound interest in, and concern for providing worldwide support for the Orthodox Church & her missionary outreach. This was especially true in regards to preserving the Holy Orthodox Church for future generations. Furthering this important mission now would certainly be a top priority for Tsar-Martyr Nicholas and his entire family.

On behalf of our rector, administration, faculty and students, I would like to thank you in advance for any and all donations you may make to our seminary. Please specify that your donation is in honor of Tsar-Martyr Nicholas II. These donations will go towards funding academic scholarships, hopefully annually. Please do not hesitate to contact me directly relative to any other questions about this worthy project, or regarding additional opportunities we have available for donors as well. My e-mail address is 'mpavuk@hts.edu'. We also invite and encourage you to visit our historic seminary and monastery in person.

Love in Christ,

— FATHER DEACON MICHAEL PAVUK
Director of Development
Holy Trinity Orthodox Seminary
Jordanville, New York

The Russian Orthodox Three-Bar Cross

The three-bar Russian Orthodox Cross eternally honors and represents the Holy Trinity — Father, Son, and Holy Spirit — that Tsar-Martyr Nicholas II put first in his life and death.

The top bar represents the title board Pontius Pilate ordered hung above our Lord and Saviour Jesus Christ's head to mock him. The middle bar is that on which His precious hands were nailed; while the letters IC XC signify the first and last letters of Christ's name in Greek. The bottom bar or footrest is slanted to represent the "balance of righteousness." On the left side of Christ, the unrepentant, hell-bound thief (downward end) and on the right side the wise, heaven-bound thief (upper end) who repented before Christ on the cross.

When the Holy Royal Martyrs were first sequestered at the Ipatiev House, the family was able to look out the windows of their second story quarters to see a Russian Orthodox Church which had three-bar crosses on its rooftop. Later, because a main road passed by the Ipatiev House, the windows were covered up so no one could see the family from outside, and they could no longer see the Church which had greatly comforted them.

This particular Orthodox Cross was fashioned by the author's father, Aleksandar Trifunovic, who enjoyed tinkering in his at-home metal-smith's workshop. It was there he made this cross for his family a few years before he died, for Pascha (Easter) 1976. It has been used since then for every one their family's weddings, baptisms, and funerals in their beloved Orthodox Church.

Contents

Tsar Nicholas II in Imperial Regalia

Myrrh-Streaming icon of Tsar-Martyr Nicholas II of Russia. He is in full regal attire flanked by Saint Nicholas of Myra (his namesake) and Saint Job the Long Suffering, on whose feast day Nicholas was born. (Commissioned by Ija Schmit)

Holy Russia, The New or Third Rome

The Imperial Crowning of a Russian Tsar represents an ancient and direct continuation of the tradition of the Christian Roman Empire (Byzantium). During the 1896 holy coronation, Tsar-Martyr Nicholas II himself, took the crown from the Metropolitan's hands and placed it upon his own head in true Byzantine Emperor custom.

Then the Metropolitan or Patriarch confirms "Imperial Supremacy" during a coronation with this spoken prayer:

"Most God-fearing, absolute, and mighty Lord, Tsar of all the Russias, this visible and tangible adornment of thy head is an eloquent symbol that thou, as the head of the whole Russian people, art invisibly crowned by the King of kings, Christ, with a most ample blessing, seeing that He bestows upon thee entire authority over His people."

+ + +

"Two Romes have fallen (Rome and Constantinople). The third stands (Russia). And there not be a fourth. No one will replace your Christian Tsardom!"

— Abbot Philotheus

Spaso-Eleazar Monastery, Pskov, Russia
1460-1542

Coronation Prayer

Spoken by Tsar-Martyr Nicholas II at his coronation.

"You, my Master and Lord, instruct me in every deed that You lay before me. Make me wise and direct me in this great service. Let the Wisdom that sits at the right hand of Your throne be with me. Let my heart be in your hand, that I may turn everything to the benefit of the people You have given me, and to Your glory."

Tsar-Martyr Nicholas II of Russia
1868-1918

Dedication

"This book was specifically written for Christ's sake, as a small, heartfelt gift to God to thank Him for giving us the most honorable and noblest and brightest of servants: the last Tsar of Russia and his family."

— Ariane Trifunovic Montemuro

I dedicate my book to the Right-believing Royal Passion-bearer Tsar-Martyr Nicholas II, of Russia. I wrote this book to fulfill a debt of love owed to him and his beloved Martyr family. The world rejected this God-ordained Tsar and left him and his God-loving family to be mercilessly slaughtered. The suffering image of Old Testament Saint Job overshadowed his life. Nonetheless, he still accepted the will of God in all his life circumstances.

During their lifetimes, Tsar-Martyr Nicholas II and his family exemplified the Beatitudes: the teachings of our Lord and Saviour, Jesus Christ. His Holy Imperial family lived out the Gospel teachings as long as they had breadth. Over 100 years after his death, this Great Tsar-Martyr would be proud to know the church bells are ringing again across Russia. Icons are back up in homes and church walls. Today, the legacy of his life as Tsar-Martyr of Russia has become a source of constant inspiration for us all.

In an oftentimes Godless world, the Tsar-Martyr shows us how to follow Jesus Christ. Even though the atheists murdered this pious and good last Romanov Tsar, his death was not in vain. His bright Godly life and family legacy continues to grow now that he has become a Saint.

From generation to generation, the Tsar-Martyr continues to touch people from around the world to strive to put God first in all things. May the Right-believing Passion-bearing Tsar-Martyr Nicholas II of Russia inspire and pray for each and every reader of this book!

Having given his life for Christ, I believe he *will* intercede for us before Christ!

— ARIANE TRIFUNOVIC MONTEMURO
Nashville, Tennessee
2018

+ + +

Holy Royal Martyrs,
Tsar Nicholas II and Family,
Pray unto God for our salvation!

Foreword

BY ARCHIMANDRITE NEKTARIOS SERFES

July 4/17, 1918-2018 (dates in this format reflect the old and new calendar styles) marks the occasion of the One Hundredth Anniversary of the Holy Martyrdom of *His Imperial Majesty Tsar Nicholas II, Her Imperial Majesty Tsarina Alexandra, His Imperial Majesty Grand Duke Tsarevich Alexis, Her Imperial Highness Grand Duchess Olga, Her Imperial Highness Grand Duchess Tatiana, Her Imperial Highness Grand Duchess Maria,* and *Her Imperial Highness Grand Duchess Anastasia.* The hundredth anniversary of perhaps the most horrific martyrdom of its time was well attended with over 100,000 faithful present at the commemoration of the anniversary.

His Imperial Majesty Tsar Nicholas II, Emperor of Russia, and His wife, Her Imperial Majesty Empress Tsarina Alexandra were consecrated Sovereigns of the Great Russian Empire, May 14/26, 1896. During their lifetime, God and the people of the Empire were dearly beloved by them. In addition, their adored children were their joy and peace. However, during their lifetime revolution was at their doorstep; no one or no thing could have stopped this violent revolution against God, the Tsar of Russia, and his family, who became innocent, slaughtered lambs. The Imperial Romanov Family was a pious royal family who lived their lives with great spiritual fortitude. They are a magnificent role model of what a good and loving Christian family can be. In every day and every activity, we see holiness and goodness exemplified in their lives.

We can learn more about this quality of holiness from Saint John Maximovitch of San Francisco, who himself was born in village of Adamovks in the province of Kharkov in southern Russia. He often wrote about the Royal Martyrs Tsar Nicholas II and his family with great devotion and with love. In reflecting on the holiness of the Royal Martyrs, Saint John wrote humbly in this manner:

"Holiness is not simply righteousness, for which the righteous merit the enjoyment of blessedness in the Kingdom of God, but rather such a height of righteousness that men are filled with the grace of God to the extent that it flows from them upon those who associate with them. Great is their blessedness; it proceeds from personal experience of the Glory of God. Being filled also with love for men, which proceeds from love of God, they are responsive to men's needs, and upon their supplication they appear also as intercessors and defenders from them before God."[1]

The pursuit of holiness and righteousness, as well as love for God, was the main emphasis of the daily life of the Royal Martyrs of Russia. This pursuit took on an enhanced quality and importance once the Tsar, his beloved family, and friends were placed under house arrest, first in Tsarskoye Selo, then in Tobolsk, and finally in Ykaterinburg. In reflecting on this period of house arrest, we begin to see a heightened spirituality in their actions and in their letters sent to family members and friends. Even the young, innocent, Heir to the throne, Tsarevich Alexis expresses great humility, endurance, patience and love to those who persecuted him and his beloved family. Grand Duchess Olga expressed the need for love for all on behalf of her father the Tsar. The Empress Alexandra encouraged faith and prayer, to the recipients of her thoughtful correspondence.

While under house arrest, everything was taken away from them. Therefore, it is clear that materialism meant nothing to this devoted Godly family. We find that all the palaces and all the riches that go with a monarchy meant to them a means of loving and supporting one another, loving God — and even loving their enemies. Every member of this family knew that it was not going to be long before they would have to face an evil attack and an evil end; this was apparent in the way each one was treated on a daily basis while under house arrest. Often those who were in charge during this time had to be relieved of their posts because they themselves found this family to be most honorable, meek, innocent, kind, righteous, and loving. The Bolshevik authorities had to bring in the cruelest men to guard them, men who had no love for this family or indeed anyone else. Such men were not hard to find as Russia and its people began to turn away from the love of their own Tsar and from God, as well as from one another!

The question was, how to get rid of this family? It has been recently reported that several ideas have come to light showing how the authorities debated this issue. One was that they should blow up the Ipatiev House; another was that they could poison the family. Finally it was decided to simply shoot all the members of the Royal Family and also those devoted servants who had voluntarily gone with them into captivity, not wanting to leave them at this time of trial. No one was to escape, and not one was to live! Love was to be destroyed! Love for God, love for one another, love for country now had a different meaning! A new type of internal power was being created, and those who sought this power turned away from God, and in the end even away from their own people.

This hundredth anniversary cannot be just be forgotten or be overlooked, because God in His great Love has not allowed this righteous family to be forgotten, even among those who continue to persecute the Royal Family by their words and in the continuing assertion that this family was the reason for the fall of Russia. This is truly false.

I believe it was not just one issue, or one individual who brought the down fall of the Imperial Romanov family, but that it was a combination of many historical factors, as well as serious decline in the spirituality of the Russian people. One cannot blame just the Tsar, the Tsarina, the Tsarevich, or the Grand Duchesses, or any other influences, because we have to look at the whole picture and contemporary accounts of the times. Too many false accounts were presented by the Bolshevik Government and then the Communist Party. The media did not help either, nor did those who betrayed the Imperial Romanov Family. Insiders and outsiders were hungry for power and domination. Those who finally did take complete control of the government and Russian people did not believe in God; they were motivated by different, materialistic principles. Sadly enough, since the fall of communism in Russia, we still encounter those who have not let go of such ideals and beliefs. This is apparent among some members of the Duma, and in a certain percentage of the general population. We still have those who say that they would refuse to celebrate this hundredth anniversary of the martyrdom of Tsar Nicholas II and his family, and that they would rather have July 4/17, 2018 pass as quickly as possible.

*Father Nektarios Serfes (right)
presents one of Ariane's paintings to
Abbess Anastasia of Devič monastery in Kosovo-Metohija.*

*"The debt the Serbian people owe to Russia…
is a debt of love."*

— St. Nikolai Velimirović, Apostle from Lelić
Painting by the author.

However those who continue to love God, one another, and the Royal Martyrs of Russia, will, as they reflect on the importance of this day, gain much spiritual insight. Think about what each member of the family said and went through for the sake of all Russia and its people they loved dearly. As I have stated earlier, this spiritual heightening becomes quite apparent once the Imperial Romanov family were placed under house arrest in Tobolsk and then in Ykaterinburg. Please note that the family's actions were motivated by the greatest Christian principles, and they were a good and pure examples of the Holy Orthodox faith. They all deeply loved and believed and practiced this faith. In the end it became their strength, their hope, their joy, and their peace.

I am honored to recommend this valuable and spiritually edifying book by Ariane Trifunovic Montemuro. Ariane's book, ***Debt of Love***, reflects her lifelong admiration and love for these wonderful Saints. I pray Ariane's meaningful and deeply heartfelt book on the Royal Martyrs touches the heart of each reader. I believe it will. As a result, my hope and prayer is that each person will cultivate a personal friendship, love for, and an ongoing prayer life with these Holy Royal Martyrs of Russia.

May Ariane's love and devotion for each of these Holy Royal Martyrs be contagious! They are a source of spiritual nourishment for all who call upon them. Acquire an icon of them in your home and remember to call upon them in prayer! An icon of this family in your home will inspire one to commune with these Saints. It is time to open your hearts and make a connection with them. I encourage you to begin to learn about your *new friends*: The Holy Royal Martyrs of Russia!

Having given their lives for Christ, this last Imperial family of Russia can intercede for us all before Christ. We must continually look to the example of their lives for encouragement and strength. You may find that one of these Royal Martyrs may draw you in more than another for help with a particular life struggle. If so, commune with this Saint. Remember, at the very moment you are reading these words; these Saints you are reading about are fully alive in Paradise. They have a closeness and special boldness before the Lord, since they have fought the good fight and finished the race. So why not ask these Holy Royal Martyrs to pray for you in general or for a specific need you might have? They are alive in Christ!

Read Ariane's book, ***Debt of Love***, and I believe you will begin to call upon these new holy friends in heartfelt prayer and supplication. In turn, they will hear your prayers. These holy people the Lord calls His friends.

"You are My friends if you do whatever I command you. No longer do I call you servants, for a servant does not know what his master is doing; but I have called you friends, for all things that I heard from My Father I have made known to you." (John 15: 14-15 KJV)

Let me humbly close with this:

The following words were quoted by Saint John Maximovitch of San Francisco: *"Tsar Nicholas II was a servant of God by his inner world-outlook, by conviction, by his actions; and he was thus in the eyes of the whole Orthodox Russian people. The battle against him was closely bound up with the battle against God and faith. In a word, he became a Martyr with his family, having remained faithful to the Ruler of those who rule, and accepted death in the same as the martyrs accepted it."*

The voices of the Royal Martyrs Tsar Nicholas II and his Family are now crying out for us in prayer before the Throne of our Gracious God who loves us when we love Him and one another.

— Archimandrite Nektarios Serfes
St. Sava Award recipient 2015
President of the Decani Monastery Relief Fund

+ + +

Holy Royal Martyrs,
Tsar Nicholas II and Family
Pray unto God for us!
Glory be to God for all things!

Archimandrite Nektarios Serfes holding an icon of the Holy Royal Martyrs.

The author with her portrait of Tsar-Martyr Nicholas II, which has been blessed by Hieromonk Anatoly of Holy Trinity Monastery, Jordanville, New York.

Introduction

"Devotion and love for my true friends"

+ + +

"A true friend prays to God for his friend. A true friend cares about the salvation of a friend's soul. To draw a friend back from false ways and set him on the true path — that is a precious friendship. The Saints of God are man's greatest friends."

— Saint Nikolai Velimirović

A Debt of Love

I wrote this simple book with two intentions in mind. The first was to inspire people through my book to help the great cause of preserving our Holy Orthodox Faith for future generations. You can do so by making a charitable donation in honor of Tsar-Martyr Nicholas II of Russia. The donation would go to the Seminarian fund or to the Seminary itself at Holy Trinity, Jordanville, New York. My dream is that together we can fund a scholarship named after Tsar-Martyr Nicholas II, in honor of his beautiful family. If you are inspired by my book, please donate, and be sure to specify that your donation is in honor of Tsar-Martyr Nicholas II.

It is a much needed cause. Our faith will only survive if we have the clergy to pastor our faithful. A cause like this is one I believe the Tsar himself would have wholeheartedly supported. So if you love the Tsar-Martyr; love the faith he guarded during his reign. Donate today to Holy Trinity Seminary. Remember to make sure to include a note that your donation is to be in honor of Tsar-Martyr Nicholas II. For more information, see pages xix.

My second intention in writing this book is to express my sincere love for them. I have admired the Tsar and his family pretty much my whole life. I was in awe of them even before they were recognized as Saints. My admiration stemmed from their inner and outer beauty — both individually and also as a family of Saints. They have inspired me in more ways than I can express. These feelings of mine became so strong that I felt I had to write a personal testimony of love for them. By presenting my feelings openly, I can pay back on this spiritual "debt of love" and respect I feel I owe them. These Russian Passion-Bearing martyrs were executed together on July 4/17 (old/new calendar date styles), 1918. These Martyrs and Saints are my *true friends*. I owe them. Even today they continue to guide and inspire me on my path to salvation. Their God-loving lives provide examples for us to follow. I am eternally grateful and forever indebted to each of them! May we all follow in their footsteps of holiness.

There are four more individuals the Russian Orthodox Church outside of Russia also recognizes as Martyrs: Family Doctor Evgeni Botkin, Family Cook Ivan Kharitonov, Attendant Aleksey Trupp and Attendant Anna Demidova all perished with the Imperial family and all are recognized as Passion-Bearers with the Feast Day of July 17th. I will not be covering them in this book even though I respect and venerate them also.

Here I am, a half a world away from Russia writing this book about the last Tsar of Russia and his beloved family:

Tsar Nicholas II
Empress Alexandra
Grand Duchess Olga
Grand Duchess Tatiana
Grand Duchess Maria
Grand Duchess Anastasia
Tsarevich Aleksei

Russia and many other places in the world just celebrated the historic one-hundred year memorial (1918-2018) of the brutal execution of the entire family and its loyal attendants in Ekaterinburg, Russia. I am not Russian, nor have I ever been to Russia. Although I must admit, I deeply desire to go one day.

So, why do I feel such a strong pull to write about this final Royal Romanov dynasty family who tragically perished together in 1918 at a home named Ipatiev house? I guess my lifelong love for them will always remain a mystery to me. All I know is that they are a significant part of who I am.

The Romanov dynasty in Russia lasted over 300 years after being founded in 1613 by Mikhail Romanov at a Monastery named Ipatiev. Yes, you read that right. It began and ended at places with the same name: Ipatiev. Talk about Divine Providence. There are no accidents in God.

I have loved Tsar Nicholas II and his family since I was 11 years old. This was a time when I began to study about my favorite ballerina Anna Pavlova, who danced in the Tsar's Russian Imperial Ballet. I studied ballet seriously as a young girl and into my late teens — so it was only natural for me to fall in love with Anna Pavlova, who had danced for the Imperial family. She was a Russian ballerina who lived in Russia during the reign of Tsar Nicholas II. As I studied her life, I could not help but fall in love with the Russian Royal family as well. It was obvious to me when I read about Anna Pavlova that she loved and respected her Tsar and his family. I followed her lead. My introduction to them occurred back in the mid-to-late 1970s, a time when many lies and propaganda were floating around about them.

Why would I continue to have a lifelong love and interest in their lives and faithfully continue to study their pictures? Even recently, I felt compelled to paint Tsar-Martyr Nicholas II's likeness in oil on canvas. My interest in this family seems puzzling on the surface. Even beyond that, I feel an obligation, and maybe even a duty, to tell people exactly who they were. I find myself defending them when people say a negative word about any of them. I felt this way even as a young girl. It was almost as if they were my family. Well, in a way they all are. We share the same family of faith: Orthodox Christianity.

Most importantly, I want to remind people that they have become *Saints*. They have an important spiritual role for us all to know about. The Holy Orthodox Church has decided *they are Saints*. I always admired them. However now, I like to think of them as my new friends in heaven. I can call upon these Saints for help — and I do! They can intercede on the Throne of God for us all. In turn, because they are Saints, we can pray to them and confide in them, and ask for help, anytime and anywhere.

More than anything, my intention with this book is to express my sincere love and gratitude towards these Saints. I owe them a debt of love and gratitude. By the way, I am not a historian. This is a personal story — so you will hear a lot of how I feel about them. There are a lot of *"my feelings"* described in this book. They are my family members — so to speak! Please keep this perspective in mind as you read. Maybe you will be inspired and begin to feel this personal connection and love for them, too! Maybe one of these Saints will become a beloved friend for you!

This book is a love story. It is my small attempt to try to make a payment towards the debt of love I feel for this exceptional family. I want to give back to them my love and thanks by hopefully inspiring others to get to know them better. Now that they are Saints we can all have a relationship with them. We can include them in our prayer life. They have inspired me more than I can say. My book is my small offering of payback. I am paying back the hope and inspiration they still give us by showing us all how to live a Godly life.

These Saints are brilliant jewels on the crown of Christianity. In all they did, they always set forth Christian examples for us to follow. By studying this family of Saints you will see all the fruits of the Holy Spirit in action: love, joy, peace, patience, kindness, goodness, faithfulness, gentleness, and self-control. Because they are Saints, the good news is: *we can pray to them*! They are available to help and guide us to put God first. Their holy lives lead us on the path to salvation if we open our hearts to remembering them.

Think about it. They were one of the most powerful families on earth, but their love for each other was simple, pure, and devoted. Traditional values were the cornerstone of their family life. They loved simple pleasures. They loved God. You could see it in all their ways. Their rooms were filled with icons. Pictures abound of them practicing their Holy Orthodox Faith. The Tsar blessed the troops with holy images of our Lord and Savior Jesus Christ while he was on bent knee — or on horseback. The family was photographed coming in and out of Church. They kept the feast days and fasts. They attended the glorification (canonization) of Saints. The proof is all in the pictures. There are a multitude of photographs we have to reflect upon. We can all see the truth with our own eyes. We just need to look.

In terms of looking back, it's easy for me to pinpoint my initial love for Russia and its people — even before my ballet days. Most people of my generation with Serbian-born parents grew up with a natural affection for Russia. It kind of goes without saying, we just love Russia. After all, we share the same faith: Orthodox Christianity. This gives us the same measuring stick to analyze the world with. Serbs relate to Russians. Even our Serbian Saints loved to talk about how they love Russia and the Tsar.

In the words of Serbian Saint Nikolai Velimirović:

+ + +

"Our debt to Russia is great. A person could owe a debt to another person, a nation-to another nation. But the debt the Serbian people owe to Russia for its actions in 1914 is so great that it won't be repaid in generations or centuries. This is a debt of love, when one dies saving one's neighbor. There is no greater love than to lay down one's life for one's friends, said Christ. The Russian Tsar and Russian people, who went to war in order to defend Serbia, entered it unprepared, knowing full well that they [were] facing death. But the love the Russians have for their brothers did not retreat in the face of danger and was not afraid of death."[2]

Serbs not only loved the Tsar and his family, they admired and respected him. They still do. That's the kind of feeling I grew up with. In fact, my mother Danica described herself as a self-proclaimed Russophile quite often. She wrote this description of herself in the inside cover of a Russian book she gave me and my husband. It was one of many Russian books my mother chose for me.

Danica's gift to her daughter and son-in-law.
"To Ariane and Tony, Happy Slava, Saint Petka, 1999!
Your Russophile Mama, Danica V. Dobrich Trifunovic"

So, that's my back-story growing up Serbian-American, and you probably imagine that I have lots and lots of Russian books. Well, you are right — I do! There have been many books written about the last Tsar and his family, and I have lots of those, too. But many of these books tell about their short lives. Good, bad, and ugly words have been written. Insignificant things have been written. Anything to sell a book or two. Propaganda and betrayal, as well as far-fetched fiction, has swirled around their names even when they were living. In fact, I am hard-pressed to think of a world leader who has been so misunderstood and misrepresented as Tsar Nicholas II of Russia and his family.

Let us look together and renew our study of this beautiful Imperial family who have together become Saints — only this time let's look with "the eyes of faith." Try to imagine them living pious lives in their worldly position and the threat they were (and still are) to satan! We will see them for who they really were as Orthodox Christians. Let us now perceive them as the purely-Christian family that they were. They were pure-hearted and radiant with good deeds. Even in their most difficult days they strove to accept God's will and to love others as Christ loves. They were constantly challenged by the devil, but they fought back with the Gospel. They truly loved *The Beatitudes of Christ*. In fact, they perfectly illustrated their love of this scripture with their righteous lives.

If we perceive them with our spiritual eyes, they will truly become our heavenly friends. Then, we can turn to them in prayer and confide in them and exclaim:

O' Holy Royal Passion-Bearing Martyrs, Pray to God for us sinners, and lead us on the path to salvation!

I thank God for the fact that the truth is now coming out on these beautiful Saints! Hopefully my humble and very personal love story inspires and touches you. Maybe you'll feel prompted to learn more. If so, there are some wonderful books available. The more you learn, the more you can love!

So, now it's time for my love story. Sit down and pour yourself a cup of coffee or tea. Let's get to know who they were and who they are. I will begin to share a few of the reasons why I love this Imperial Russian family that became Saints. My hope is that the love I share is contagious and caught by you! If so, pass this book on to someone who does not know them or questions why they are now recognized as Saints. This way we can all work together and can begin to pay back *"A Debt of Love", to the Holy Royal Martyrs.* If we all join together I pray they will most certainly feel our love for them in heaven!

Finally, I would like to offer a special heartfelt thank you to Father Nektarios Serfes for all the material he contributed. His great love of these Saints inspired me to love them even more!

The author was eleven years old the first time she read about Prima Ballerina Anna Pavlova of the Tsar's Russian Imperial Ballet. When asked about the Tsar in a March 6, 1910 interview in the New York Times, *"Mlle. Pavlova repeated, her dark eyes half smiling, half surprised, 'Have I ever seen the Czar? … Why, he stroked my hair when I was a pupil—he praised me. He used to come to our school and talk to us and tell jokes and eat dinner with us — the same things we used to eat. I remember the performance the children gave in his honor.' "*

Chapter One

HOLY OIL,
THE HOLY ROYAL MARTYRS

"Blessed are the poor in spirit,
for theirs is the kingdom of Heaven."
Matthew 5:3 (KJV)

This bottle of Holy Oil, The Holy Royal Martyrs, was given to the author by Father Benedict of Holy Cross Monastery, in Wayne, West Virginia, by way of the Saints' intervention and the author's friend, Kathleen. The Holy Royal Martyrs icon was given to the author by The Very Reverend Father Stephen Rogers, years before this book had even been born as an idea. On the back, he inscribed it. "To Ariane: with much love and appreciation for your love of God and His church. Fr. Stephen."

Holy Oil, The Holy Royal Martyrs

"Blessed are the poor in spirit,
for theirs is the kingdom of Heaven."

We all know certain people can end up defining your life. They can leave an indelible imprint on your inner spiritual psyche. They can influence your thoughts and inspire you to be a better person. They become role models for you. Most of all, you deeply appreciate and respect the example of their lives. If fact, you've admired and loved these people most of your life. What if one day these people became Saints? Well, that's what this story is about. An Imperial family of Holy Saints that I truly love.

I swore I would never write another book. One was enough for me. I wrote my last book for my kids and future generations. It is called *I Shall Remember Thy Holy Name From Generation to Generation… A Serbian-American Woman Awakens to Christ's Call.* (This book is available from all major on-line booksellers.) I wanted my children to know that their Orthodox Christian heritage came from Serbia, so I wrote a book and thought *that's the end of that project*! After six years of compiling it, I finished and decided one book was enough of stepping outside my comfort zone. Especially enough for someone who views herself as an artist and not an author. But God has His own plans for our lives. We think we are in control, but we're not.

In fact, my kids and husband gave me a joint look of surprise when I announced that I would be writing another book. I even questioned myself. Who am I to write about the last Russian Imperial family of the Romanov Dynasty? Not only were they an Imperial family, but now they are Saints! They became Saints in a long drawn-out process that started in 1981 here in the United States and ended in Russia in 2000. There are already a multitude of books about them. So what made me think I should or even could write another? The passion to do it hit me like a tidal wave. I could not run from it. Suddenly I knew I had to do it — but doubt crept in. Then I began to talk to them and pray to them: *I love you all and I want to tell the world why*. In addition, I feel passionately about using this book to raise awareness for Orthodox Christian seminarians in financial need at Holy Trinity Seminary in Jordanville, New York, for whom government financial assistance is not an option. I just knew in my heart God could use this book to raise awareness for these struggling Seminarians. We need to step in. We need more Orthodox clergy. We need to see our Orthodox faith grow and continue from generation to generation! In my heart, I felt certain

Tsar-Martyr Nicholas would rally behind helping these needy Seminarians and even maintaining the Seminary itself. The book would be the vehicle to raise awareness and — through their prayers — the Tsar-Martyr and his Holy family would inspire people to donate to this worthy cause.

So could you help me? I prayed to Tsar-Martyr Nicholas. *Please intercede on the throne of God. I would like to write this book.* Again my doubts crept in. *How can I express my love for them in a way people will relate to?* I am not an expert in anything; I only know that I truly love them. I turned towards heaven in my heart and prayed to Tsar-Martyr Nicholas again: Please Tsar-Martyr, I am not sure. *Please Tsar-Martyr, could you pray for me for me, and could you ask the Lord to help me if it is His will for me to do this?*

I continued to pray, and then I attended my first Divine Liturgy after I made my not-so-confident decision to write another book. I prayed again, this time directly to God as I fixed my eyes and heart upon his icon in church. *Help me, Lord, only if this is Your will.* Then I turned to the icon of the Theotokos, Most Holy Mother of God, and implored of Her: *Please ask your Son to show me if it's His will that I should write another book.* I kept on praying. *Guide me Lord, give me the confidence to write a book on these Saints I love, because I really want to!* My prayers kept coming out of my heart — one after another — and then Divine Liturgy ended and so did my prayers to write another book.

I collected my things, and as I was leaving church my friend Kathleen said, "Wait, Ariane. I have something for you." She reached into her purse and pulled out a small bottle and the label on it said, *Holy Oil, The Holy Royal Martyrs.* I was completely stunned, and I could not believe it! I hugged her in thanks. Kathleen then said, "It's from Father Benedict at Holy Cross Monastery, in Wayne, West Virginia." (Some of you may not have heard of the beautiful new shrine and reliquary of the Holy Royal Martyrs recently installed at the monastery. This was one of several gifts from an anonymous benefactor.) My friend continued her story. "We were just visiting the Monastery, and he asked me to give it to you, Ariane." Filled with surprise and even disbelief, I took her gift. Bewildered but grateful, I turned to her and joyfully hugged her a second time thanking her. As she walked away, I said *thank you, God,* whispering to myself and smiling. *I think I'll be writing another book.*

I wonder what the odds of that were. Until that day, no one at my church knew of my sudden desire to write this book on the Holy Royal Romanov Passion-Bearers of Russia. However, the Saints knew. They knew what I was up to. So, I was given a little miracle, and my confidence grew. Not because suddenly I gained some sort of wisdom. Trust me, I did not. It grew because I knew I was not doing this alone. I knew in my heart the Saints heard me. I knew God was with me. I also knew the Holy Royal Martyrs would pray for me. Finally, I knew I could share my love for them in a uniquely personal way. It was time to begin to write!

In fact, I have been talking to these Saints and asking for them to intercede for me for a while now. I guess using worldly terms I would call them my go-to Saints! There is something about looking at them that always inspires my faith. Honestly, some days really test my faith. Life can be hard. However, these Saints have a way of pulling me back up. Even when I feel down or alone, they are with me. I might even just ask one of them to pray for me. Each one of their beautiful souls has something special to give. They nourish me spiritually! I am an artist, therefore, I am a visual person. The large collection of photographs that remains of this Imperial family has touched me deeply. Because of these beautiful and varied photographs; I feel an even deeper bond with them. This bond has grown stronger since they have become Saints. They are called Royal Passion-Bearing Saints or Martyrs in Orthodox Christian lexicon. The 1981 glorification here in the United States refers to them as *Martyrs* and the 2000 Russian glorification refers to them as *Passion-Bearers*. Because I am just a layperson and not a theologian, I may respectfully switch back and forth indicating who they are; but you'll know what I mean!

It's amazing and wonderful that the Romanov family were avid photographers. You can even see them holding cameras in many photos! It is mind boggling that you can actually see the whole history of their lives in beautiful photographs. That's a rare treasure to enjoy! Because of these photos you can even see how their strong likenesses were eventually translated into icons. Icons are holy and theological images created specifically for veneration in the Orthodox Church and are not considered works of art.

We can venerate them through icons in Church but also get to know them better through photography. I am particularly drawn to their informal family photos as well as the ones in which they illustrate their faith. Those are the photos I will highlight in this book. It's also a joy to look at the informal photos they took of each other. These favorite everyday-life pictures of this beloved God-loving family pull me right into the story of their lives from joy to sadness. They speak to me, and I believe they will speak to you.

I was an art history major in college and I remember my coursework on the history of photography and found it quite interesting. Printed photographs began to be available to the general public around the mid-19th century. After that, progress in photo equipment made it affordable to the public, and as a result, there was a global photo revolution. Everyone began the hobby of taking pictures, including the Tsar and his family. As you can imagine, the Romanov Imperial family would have had access to the best and most modern equipment, such as the U.S.-made Kodak camera. The photos are black and white, and many are of very good quality. They are quite clear and candid and are a poignant visual history of their lives. A history that we can study as we attempt get to know these Saints better.

There is an old saying: 'The Camera cannot lie.' At least that was true back then, before we had the ability to edit the photographic image. The idea behind the phrase is that a photo was always a true and faithful representation of a subject. On the other hand, a painting is subjective. A painting may have the influence of the artist's opinions or feelings represented. Trust me, I know about that. I am an artist; an oil painter, in fact. Unlike an iconographer, for an example, I do insert my opinions into what I paint. My paintings tell the story I want to tell. Photographs can be infallible and precise records of a subject. I do believe this is especially true with our subjects during this particular time in history in which they lived: the early twentieth century. At this time, photographs were not generally manipulated to tell another story. A photograph recreated exactly what was in front of the camera at a particular moment in time.

The Royal Couple with cameras.

Young Tsarevich Aleksei holding a camera.

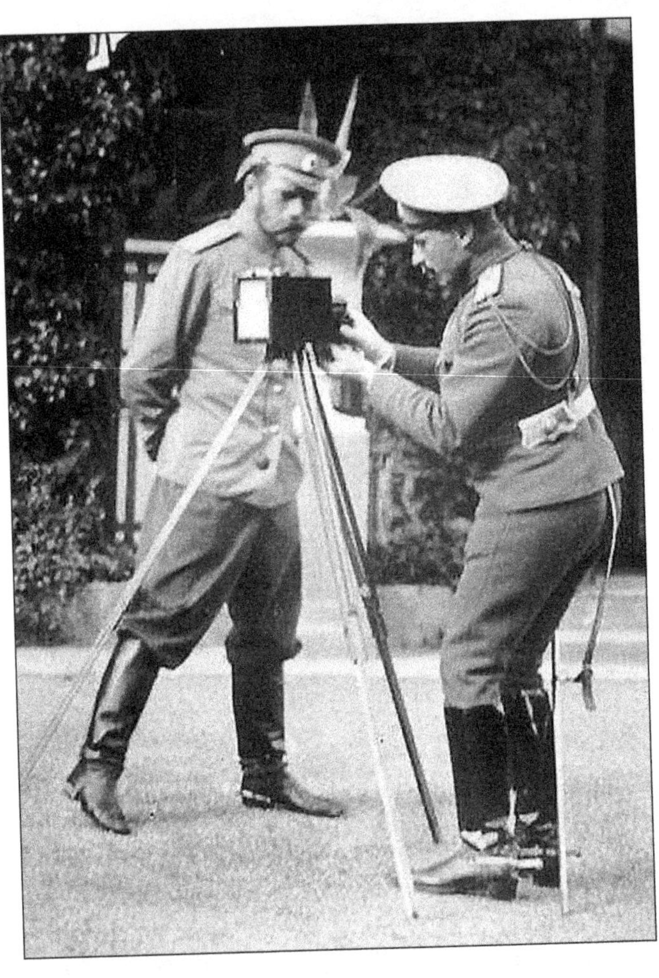

The Tsar observing the photographic process.

The Tsarina with camera.

The Grand Duchess Anastasia taking an early selfie.

The Grand Duchess Tatiana holding a camera with her sisters and mother.

In order to truly see this family in the correct light you must understand the Orthodox Christian faith they practiced and the time in history in which they lived. The start of the twentieth century was undoubtedly one that expressed the most remarkable technological innovations and discoveries. The list is endless: radio broadcasting, telephones, electricity, automobiles are just some of the new century innovations. So many changes were being introduced into society and not all of these innovations were material. Some were spiritual. Anti-Christian ideas and philosophies were also seeping into their Imperial Russian homeland at a record pace. Theosophy and spiritualism were some of these. People were practicing table-tipping to connect with so-called supernatural forces. Communicating with the dead was in. In Europe and America these occult interests were spreading throughout society. It is widely known that foreign ideas and occult forces were behind the Bolshevik Revolution. The symbols of the Soviet regime, the hammer, the sickle, and the star are symbols of the post-Christian age.

Bolsheviks were anti-God and therefore, anti-Holy Russia. Theirs was an all-out spiritual war with the Tsar because of who he took his leadership from. Their chief aim was to dismantle Holy Russia bit by bit. *Remember the Holy Tsar represented Holy Rus' or Holy Russia*. Almighty God was and is the Lord of All in Russia. In turn, Russia's unique history is Orthodox Christian. Its aim as a nation was to strive to be Holy, not only in word but also in deed. The

Tsar was there to lead the way and maintain a Holy Russia! The Russian Orthodox Church expresses itself as both human and divine. It's pretty simple: humans follow the divine, the divine being the Kingdom of God. In the "Poem about the book of the Mysteries," (Golubinaia Kniga), we read these words: "Holy Rus' is a land that is mother to all lands, Apostolic churches are built on her. They pray to the crucified God, to Christ Himself, the King of Heaven. Therefore, holy-Rus-land is the mother to all lands." Furthermore, a service to all Russian Saints (composed in 1918), has probably the most famous use of this passage: *O' Holy Russia! Preserve the Orthodox Faith!* [3] Tsar Nicholas II and Tsarina Alexandra were raising their Orthodox Christian family and ruling their vast Holy Russian empire during the onset of this century.

Tsar Nicholas II was born near St. Petersburg, in Tsarskoye Selo, (now Pushkin) Russia on May 6/18, 1868, the day of Holy Job the Long-Suffering. What a day to be born! St. Job the Righteous was God's faithful servant in the Bible, the perfect image of every virtue one can think of! The Tsar-Martyr was born with the perfect name-day Saint, considering his own righteous character and his future terrible burdens in life. God gave him the ideal Saint. The young Nicky or future Tsar Nicholas II went on to inherit the throne when his father, Alexander III died in 1894. He grew up immersed in his Holy Russian Orthodox heritage of beautiful churches and monasteries and of Holy Saints and Martyrs. His character was fully formed in his ancient homeland, one filled with a rich spiritual tradition and history of ancient Byzantine Iconography, spiritual books, and sacred church music.

One day in 1917, the militant Bolshevik atheists seized complete power and everything changed. Not long after that, the God-loving Tsar and his family were held together in captivity, and after a time, mercilessly executed. Holy Russia was gone. The Imperial Romanov Dynasty was dismantled. Churches and monasteries were looted and stripped bare and routinely destroyed. Russian Orthodox Christianity, the official religion of the Tsar and Holy Russia, became a faint memory. If you were connected to the church or had any kind of Imperial Russian connections, you were pretty much done for. Countless monks and priests were murdered. Anything or anyone with ties to the Tsar was snuffed out. Religion became a joke under the new atheist regime. Pious religious folk became the target.

Let's face it, even a non-historian, everyday person like me can clearly see the Bolshevik revolution was an all-out revolution against God. There was no place for God in the new Soviet Union. So, naturally, the Tsar, who was "God's- Anointed," had no place either. He was done for, and everyone associated with him had the same fate. God was out and the satan was in. Simply put, it was *atheist revolution*.

You've probably already guessed by now that I am not going to portray them simply as Royals. No palace intrigues and jewel stories here. Futhermore, I am not going to write about some far-fetched fake conspiracy theory. Since we share the same Orthodox Christian faith, I understand how to present them as who they really were: a God-loving family that believed God's will created and chose them to be the Russian Imperial family. If I — an everyday non-scholar — can see them as they truly were, then anyone can. All you need are eyes to see and a heart to perceive. God gave us all the gift of this beautiful hope-filled Christian family.

In fact, many refer to the last Tsar Nicholas II as, the "God-Anointed Tsar." So let's put the spotlight on this Saint and talk about what that really means. How is it that the Tsar is called: *"God-Anointed?"* I think the best person to answer this question is another Saint.

Why was Tsar Nicholas II persecuted, slandered, and killed? Saint John Maximovitch asked this question and then answered it for us clearly. He said the following words remembering the Royal Martyrs (long before they became Saints) in July 1963, the forty-fifth anniversary of their martyrdoms:

"Because he was Tsar, Tsar by the Grace of God. He was the bearer and incarnation of the Orthodox world view that the Tsar is the servant of God, the Anointed of God, and that to Him he must give account for the people entrusted to him by destiny, for all his deeds and actions, not only those done personally, but also as a Tsar..."[4]

To sum it all up, he viewed his Tsar's crown as a service to God. He always kept this duty in mind in everything he did. This included his personal life as a husband and a father. You could also see him with clergy at the official blessing to open the State Duma (legislative assembly) or with an icon blessing his troops and there are many more examples. God was included in everything the Tsar did in his reign. God was not forgotten. In fact God was first. Not many books highlight this fact! But it's right in front of us to see. We just have to stop and *look* at the photos of this Tsar during his rule. God was the head of his Imperial realm and after that came Tsar Nicholas the II. The Tsar was there to promote and do God's will. The Tsar's Minister of Foreign Affairs, Alexander Petrovich Izvolsky wrote the following about an armed revolt that broke out in mid-July 1906, in Kronstadt:

"On that day, July 20, when the mutiny had reached its culminating point, I was by the Emperor in Peterhof… The line of reinforcements could be seen from the window… We clearly heard the sound of the canons… I could not detect the slightest sign of agitation in his features… After the briefing the Emperor said: If you see me in such a calm state, this is because I have an unshakable faith that the fate of Russia, my own fate and the fate of my family are in the Lord's hands. No matter what happens, I will bow before His will."[5]

Wow, what a virtue. Tsar Nicholas II was poor in spirit. He could have been prideful and thought he was "all that" because he was the Tsar. Instead, he knew he was nothing without God. His will, his ego, his pride were totally empty and his heart was been made open for His Creator. The only thing I can perceive in this is the Tsar knew he was nothing except by the grace of God. I certainly could stand to learn from his example. This Ruler bowed his will before God's will and by doing so, glorified His Holy Name. Therefore, he was upholding the idea of a Holy Russia.

I am nothing compared to the Tsar. I have no Royal genes. I am an everyday woman who will only be remembered one day — hopefully — by my children and grandchildren when I am long gone. But I cannot even come close to having a faith like the Tsar did. I would be freaking out if the troops were coming! I would not be calm. I would be scanning the exit points. I can certainly rationalize in my mind that God is always in control. But actually living this belief is another matter. I cannot honestly say that I always remember that. One thing is certain, God knew what He was doing when He picked pious Tsar Nicholas II to lead. Especially to lead spiritually before the Godless Bolshevik Revolution.

God gave us the Imperial Romanov family over one hundred years ago — future Saints — that knew how to follow His will like nobody's business. They are our role models even today, when their century is long gone. What kind of role models do we get from the world now? Slim pickings, I'd say. We need to look back and learn instead of always looking away from Saints like these. They remind us to stand for the Name of Christ, for the Church, and to have the faith to submit our wills in favor of God's will for our lives. This Tsar virtues trickled down to all his children and his wife. They humbly accepted God's will like suffering Job in the Old Testament. They all seemed to exemplify this trait that, as I mentioned, is so oftentimes impossible for me to grasp.

When I study their pure faces, talk to them, pray and venerate their icons, I begin to feel the Peace of God in my life struggles. Even their sad faces in the photos remind me of this peace and that this worldly life is not our true home. I am reminded by them constantly to seek this peace through the Gospel and accept God's will in my life. When things don't go my way, I keep on pushing and pushing — sometimes, the wrong way! I want to do my own thing. I stumble. I feel lost. I forget to ask for God's blessing to start something. I don't like the outcome of some of my life experiences or encounters, and I get angry or irritated. Many times I cannot let something go, and I want to fight the outcome. I get so worn out. Finally I let go and remember these Saints. I stop and look at their faces in my books. I decide to read about them and light a candle in front of their icon. Slowly, I begin to feel less angry, less alone. I lose my tears and my fight. They draw me back to peace. I let go and wait for God. They give me hope and set me on the true path. They remind me to involve God in all things. I see their Imperial, beautiful Saint faces in all the pictures, and they reach out to me. Their eyes speak to me. I venerate their icons with prayers and ask them each to pray for me and my family. I talk to them as true friends and tell them my worries and problems. Slowly, I sense love and peace entering my heart. I feel myself turning to face God. Everything in my life begins to become Holy and good again. Everything.

\+ + +

Chapter Two

LIKE ATTRACTS LIKE

*"Blessed are those that mourn,
for they shall be comforted."*
Matthew 5:4 (KJV)

This official hand-colored 1894 French Imperial engraving commemorates the coronation of Tsar Nicholas II and his wife Alexandra after the death of the Tsar's father, Alexander III.

Like Attracts Like

"Blessed are those that mourn for they shall be comforted."

There is an old saying, "Like attracts like." It is difficult to adequately explain my longstanding admiration for Tsar Nicholas II, and it's even more of a challenge now that the Tsar and his family have become Saints. I began to admire Tsar Nicholas II when I was a pre-teen girl — long before he was known as a Martyr. I found myself defending him and the entire Imperial family. Since I was raised by Serbian-born parents, it's not a surprise that I love the Imperial Romanov family. Historically, Serbs tend to admire and respect them. Therefore, my love for the Tsar and his family comes naturally. My mother had several books on them that I had access to growing up. They were all secular books written from a Western perspective. As a kid I did not even read these books from cover to cover; instead, I carefully studied every single one of the photos in those books. It was easy for me to fall in love with the beautiful Imperial Romanov family.

When I think about these two young lovebirds together I think of their endearing childhood nicknames. We know they were commonly referred to as Sunny and Nicky. Many people, however, do not know about the special nickname the future Tsar's grandfather gave his grandson. This grandfather was Tsar Alexander II and he himself was commonly known as the "liberator of the peasants." Tsar Alexander II loved his grandson very much and affectionately called him, "Sun Ray." Nicholas visited him every day as a child. The love was mutual. In fact, I believe little Nicky learned one of his greatest distinguishing character traits from his grandfather. *How to submit your will to God's will.*

The future Tsar (nicknamed "Sun Ray" by his grandfather Alexander II) sitting in his mother's lap. His father, Alexander III, is standing behind them, and his adoring grandfather is seated next to him.

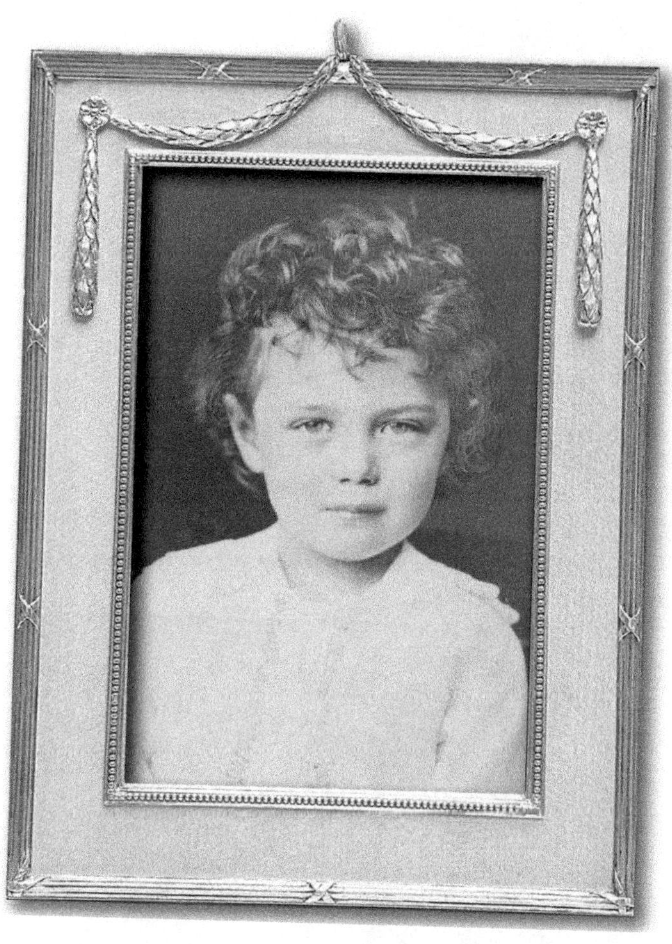

"Sun Ray," the Future Tsar Nicholas II

*Left:
Future
Tsar Nicholas II
with his mother,
Maria Feodorovna.*

Below: The future Tsar and his loving father, Alexander III.

The future Tsar with his family.

One evening young Nicholas was out with his grandfather for an all-night vigil in church. Suddenly, a ball of fiery lightning burst in through the window and was heading straight towards his beloved grandfather's head. His grandfather proceeded to cross himself. It then whirled around the floor, then passed the chandelier and then flew out through the door into the park. The young Nicholas was absolutely panic stricken. His heart froze. He then looked at his grandfather who was completely calm and crossed himself again. From that point on little Nicholas was no longer afraid of storms. He decided to believe that everything was at the mercy of God as his grandfather believed. For the rest of his life he exemplified this belief — not only with storms but with everything, it seems. Right before Tsar Alexander II died, his own son called young Nicholas to see him. He announced, "Papa, '*your Sun Ray is here.*' The Tsar opened his light blue eyes, smiled and then succumbed to mortal wounds inflicted by a revolutionary fanatic in 1881. His Sun Ray grandson was 13 years old.

I see many similarities whenever I read about the future Tsar Nicholas — Sun Ray — and the future Tsarina Alexandra — who was known as a child as Sunny — before they actually met. It's like a connect-the-dots game. They were alike not only in their nicknames Sunny and Sun Ray, but also in the depth of their youthful characters.

"Sunny," the future Tsarina Alexandra

Sun Ray and Sunny both came from large, tightly-knit, loving and pious Christian families. Nicholas' father Tsar Alexander Alexandrovich was a strong man who feared God. He became one of Russia's great Tsars — even though his reign was short (1881-1894). His mother, formerly Princess Dagmar of Denmark, was a loving and supportive wife and mother who completely embraced her adopted faith of Holy Orthodoxy. Together they transmitted the Holy Orthodox faith to their children, building their house on a rock. "And when the flood arose, the stream beat vehemently upon that house, and could not shake it: for it was founded upon a rock." (Luke 6:48)

The thread of the Tsarina's piety started young. She was nicknamed for her "Sunny" cheerful disposition as a very young child. Sunny was raised in a very pious Christian household. Tragically though, she lost her charitable and God-loving mother when she was quite young. Her mother died from diphtheria (a highly contagious and potentially life-threatening bacterial disease) when Sunny was only six years old. She lost other siblings too. The death of her mother, in particular, had to have had a deep emotional and spiritual impact on her. Whenever I study photos of her mother with her siblings, I see her mother wearing a huge cross.

The future Tsarina's mother,
wearing her cross, with her daughters.

There is another photo taken after her mother's death in which the siblings are photographed together again, but this time with their mother's portrait. I see the changes in her no-longer-Sunny face in photos after her mother's death. It really touches my heart to see this. She must have longed for her mother and spoken to her when she missed her. I know when I lost my Dad I would talk to him a lot, and I still do. Sometimes I would open his closet doors and hug his clothes before my mother gave them all away. I missed him so much! But I was eighteen and the future Tsarina was only six years old when her mother died. That must have been so terrible for her! Her young character was shaped in mourning. Her early disposition, which gave her the nickname Sunny, changed. Again, look at the photos and you can see it in her young eyes. She became more introverted and reserved after her mother's passing. I know I would have found this almost unbearable to live without my mother at only six. She experienced such a deep loss at a premature age. It no doubt made her into a different little girl. After a profound loss, you feel different because you are different. It's something that never leaves you.

The future Tsarina sitting under her mother's portrait, in mourning after her mother's death.

Queen Victoria — Queen of the United Kingdom of Great Britian and Ireland and Empress of India — and her granddaughter, The future Tsarina of Russia, in mourning for Sunny's mother, who was also the Queen's daughter.

I remember television shows and magazines I saw as a kid presenting drama-filled documentaries about them. There were always many untruths floating around concerning the family. Those stories never seemed right to me. As far back as I can remember there was a prevailing attitude of criticism against the last Imperial family of Russia. Recently, I can see from the news and reports from friends in Russia that they are loved — for the most part — in their homeland. In America, the court of public opinion is softening towards them, but even today I find many people still criticize. Some don't even understand why they have become Saints! Most of all, I find that Tsar Nicholas II is especially maligned and misunderstood. This saddens me.

I could continue by telling you more about my admiration and respect for the Tsar to vindicate him. I could present facts with my personal thoughts and defend him against untruths. I have heard terrible lies about him. His enemies have referred to him as an ignoramus, a dimwit and a bloodthirsty savage. If I hear a negative opinion about him, I am always perplexed and tongue-tied. I don't even know where to begin to reply. I could tell people he was anything but stupid, bloodthirsty, or weak — like Western propaganda has publicized. I want to shout out and exclaim to all that he spoke five languages (Russian, English, French, German, and Italian), and he was very well-educated. He was a devout Christian, a peace-loving ruler, and a pious man who totally acquiesced to the will of God. In turn, all this made him extraordinarily forgiving to others. He was courageous, charitable, and kind. He was strict with his own expenses but generous with others. I have heard several stories of his generosity helping churches here in America. I would be remiss if I didn't point out that he was a wonderfully devoted husband and family man. Finally, this was a Tsar who viewed his crown as an Imperial service to God. I could go on and on, but my opinions prove absolutely nothing.

Instead, in this time in which marriages do not last a lifetime, *his choice* of his lifetime love, "darling Sunny," as he so often addressed her in letters, strikes me as a crystal clear illustration of the spiritual depth and wisdom of his own character, because this choice says so much about him. He chose to love and marry Alix, a German Princess of Hessen-Darmstadt and a favorite granddaughter of Queen Victoria. The future Empress's Lady-in-waiting and dearest friend, Anna Virubova, wrote that no photo ever did Alix justice. You could not see her coloring and her graceful movements. She was tall and beautifully shaped. Her abundant hair, red gold, was so long when unbound that she could easily sit on it. Her complexion was clear and rosy as a little child's. She wrote that her eyes were deep gray and very lustrous. It was only later in life that sorrow and anxiety gave her eyes a melancholy. In youth they wore an expression of constant merriment. That's why her family gave her the nickname of "Sunny" growing up. This name, by the way, was nearly always used by future Tsar Nicholas II. Anna even continued to say that she began to love and admire the future Empress from the first day she met her. Then she wrote she has loved her ever since and always will.[6]

It is evident from her lady-in-waiting that it was easy to love Alix, who had to have been very special to gain such a life-long devotion from her. In fact, Anna loved her so much she dedicated her book, *Memories of the Russian Court*, to her. The cover page in her book says: "To My Empress, with love and fidelity eternal." Then she included one of her Empress's last diary entries of advice from a Saint she loved.

+ + +

"When you are reproached — bless; when persecuted — be patient; when calumniated — comfort yourself; when slandered — rejoice; this is your road and mine."

—Saint Seraphim of Sarov
1754-1833

The Tsarina with her beloved friend and lady-in-waiting Anna Virubova.

She wrote that quote to ponder upon while she was imprisoned in Tobolsk, March 20, 1918. I had to look up the word calumniated when I first read this. After I understood the meaning of the word, this line stood out to me: "When calumniated — comfort yourself." It means when someone smears you or drags your good name through the mud, comfort yourself. So this future Saint took her cues during difficult times from one of the greatest Russian ascetics and wonderworkers. Saint Seraphim of Sarov was a great follower of Christ and is now known throughout the world. Let us all remember the fact that it was Tsar Nicholas II and Tsarina Alexandra who were instrumental in pushing for his canonization (glorification). You may remember how I mentioned the Tsar was the target of lies and untruths. Well, the Tsarina was also mercilessly scandalized. Most people don't realize the depth of this woman's pious and loving character. Even at the end of her life, she looks to the Saints and keeps her eyes on Christ. She's a role model for us all. Alas, lies and personal attacks against the Tsar and Tsarina have been going on for over 100 years. My mother used to say the devil never sits still.

It's funny the random things you absorb and remember when you read. Something uniquely personal can draw you in. After I looked up the meaning of the word calumniated, I read further and saw the date of March 20th, and recognized that date as the day my father Aleksandar Trifunovic died. He passed away suddenly one Saturday morning of a heart attack. I was only 18 and a freshman in college.

I clearly remember how I was angry for a whole year. How could a good God take my father? Where is this good God for me? I was mad. I questioned God over and over. Why do the other young women have Dads to walk them down the aisle at their wedding and now I don't? I miss Daddy. I am bitter about this, God. These used to be my feelings. I kept them locked in my heart for more than a year! I had lots of diary entries elaborating upon these feelings — all about me and my own pain. I often questioned God and His motives for my young life. Never once did I read the Bible or look to a Saint's advice to find peace within my troubled soul.

I am almost stunned when I reflect upon what the Empress wrote. Unlike me, she was writing about all the virtues you should practice during your trials in life. She was not mad at God. She did not question His will. She was literally months away from a cruel death and was focused on virtues. I read nothing about her anger. She accepted God's will without question. She was a woman, an Empress, already frightened for her family, mocked and persecuted by her Bolshevik jailers. The year she wrote this quote in her 1918 notes was the year of her own and her entire family's eventual murder. There is no doubt in my mind that she must have felt a strong sense of the impending tragedy that was coming. It is commonly known that Lenin's cronies kept switching out the Bolshevik jailers for meaner and crueler ones. Each new harsh shift of jailers kept softening after spending time with such a sweet, loving family. It's difficult for me to imagine how she continued to act with such virtuous thoughts. During this frightening and seemingly hopeless time of her life she was still interested in saving quotes about practicing the virtues. Now that's a Saint's heart. To top it all off, this quote came from one of her favorite Saints — a true spiritual giant, Saint Seraphim of Sarov. She was turning to a Saint in her time of need. She certainly knew how to commune with the Saints. She knew the Saints were her true friends in Christ. Will I remember them in my time of need? I hope so.

Back to the old saying: "Like attracts like." I imagine that Nicky must have been immediately attracted to beautiful and mysterious "Sunny." Beyond her exquisite physical appearance, he must have felt her spiritual depth of character. The two met in Saint Petersburg at the wedding of Alix's older sister, Princess Elizabeth of Hesse-Darmstadt, to Nicholas' uncle, Grand Duke Sergei Alexandrovich. Nicky was smitten, it seemed, right after meeting her, and was convinced he was going to marry her. She was such a striking beauty that she quickly caught his eye and his heart. She became unforgettable to him. It had to be divine providence that those two met at the wedding of her older sister, a sister and future sister-in-law who would also become a Saint one day.

The beautiful future Tsarina and her older sister, Elizabeth.

This family is literally surrounded by future Saints! Holiness-in-the-works was everywhere to be seen! I encourage my readers to study the life of Alix's remarkable sister, the Grand Duchess Elizabeth of Russia. There is a most wonderful book on her by Lubov Millar. It's my personal favorite. Alix's sister eventually became known as Saint Elizabeth the New Martyr. She has changed so many people's lives, in so many different places. In fact, I am one of them! The life of one Saint can profoundly change a person's life. Many churches around the world are dedicated to Saint Elizabeth the New Martyr. There is a lovely church with her namesake, not far from me in Murfreesboro, Tennessee. It just goes to show the truth of one holy and bright life in Christ cannot be contained. It will eventually shine everywhere on earth.

Back to our love story: After this first meeting, their mutual and deep affections lasted a long time before they actually became a royal couple. Many years later, Nicholas proposed to Alix, however, his proposal was met with rejection. Her refusal was only due to faith considerations. She realized she would have to convert from her Lutheran faith and become Russian Orthodox in order to marry a future Tsar of Russia. It seemed she did not want to hurt her widowed father. However, in order to marry Nicholas this had to happen. After a time of intense study and heartfelt thought she agreed. She did not take her conversion lightly. In her bed-room at Tsarskoe Selo was a little door in the wall, leading to a tiny dark chapel lit by hanging lamps, where she prayed. The future Empress used to go to the Kazan Cathedral, in Saint Petersburg, where she knelt in the shadow of a pillar attended by only one lady-in-waiting. I am so touched when I imagine the Tsarina reverently doing this. For the future Tsarina, life on earth was a trial in the most literal sense. Human beings were tested to be worthy of heavenly bliss. She loved the ritual and chanting of Divine Liturgy. Her faith brought her into communion with all people, from peasant to high-born folk. She was an organized and efficient Christian philanthropist who passionately practiced her faith in the world through her multitude charitable works. Even on holiday, she toured the hospitals and sanatoriums with her young daughters. She believed that they should understand the sadness underneath all this beauty. She was no empty-headed beauty. Nicholas must have seen all her spiritual depth when he looked into her beautiful eyes.

After her conversion to Orthodoxy, life was full of transitions. They were experiencing great happiness tinged with great sadness. Nicholas' father Alexander III lay dying in terrible pain from nephritis in October, 1894. Now officially known as Alexandra (after her conversion to Orthodoxy), the future Tsarina was summoned to join the Imperial family at his bedside. The dying Tsar rose from his sickbed and, dressed in full uniform, gave her the dignity due her as a royal bride.[7] That gesture says a lot about Nicholas' father. Another thing that struck me was who he called upon at his deathbed: He chose spiritual giant Father John Kronstadt, the world-renown confessor and miracle-worker. The Tsar ended up dying on November 1, 1894. One day, many years later, on November 1, 1964, this wonderful priest would become Saint John Kronstadt. And let us not forget the future Empress Alexandra's sister. The Grand Duchess Elizabeth's birthday was also on November 1st. Now that's some holy timing! God ordains the timing of all things. We can see this in our own lives. There are no accidents in God. Everything has meaning, from the day you were born to your name. We only have to study the Bible to prove that.

As you can easily imagine by now, the future Empress regularly studied the Gospel. You know the old saying: Actions speak louder than words. Alexandra was someone who really lived out the meaning of the Gospel. She was widely known to express her faith through charitable works and active hospital work and I mean active. You could say it was in Alexandra's genes. Her own mother had founded hospitals and engaged in Red Cross work herself. Once Alexandra became a mother, she actively taught her children by example, to follow the commandment of Christ to visit the sick. Her teaching style was hands-on. She did it herself and the children followed suit. Again, study the photos and you will see the Empress dressed in her nurse's uniform aiding the sick and wounded. Look around her and you will see her children nearby. How many Empresses can you think of who did this? Her husband ruled the largest nation in the world. The Tsarina acted out of boundless love and respect for her people. She did not delegate the difficult or messy work to others. She got involved and she did the work. I wish more people knew this about her.

Anna A. Virubova wrote, “I have personally seen the Empress of Russia in the operating room, assisting in the most difficult operations, taking from the hands of the busy surgeon amputated legs and arms, removing bloody and even vermin-ridden field dressings.” Virubova says that she was “a born nurse,” and that she enormously increased the efficiency of the hospital system in Russia. I suspect not many people know this about her, either.

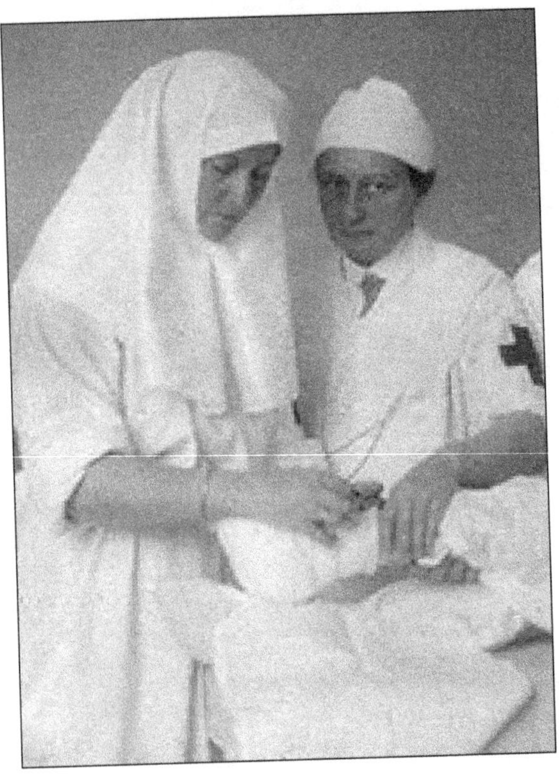

The Tsarina personally aiding the wounded during WWI.

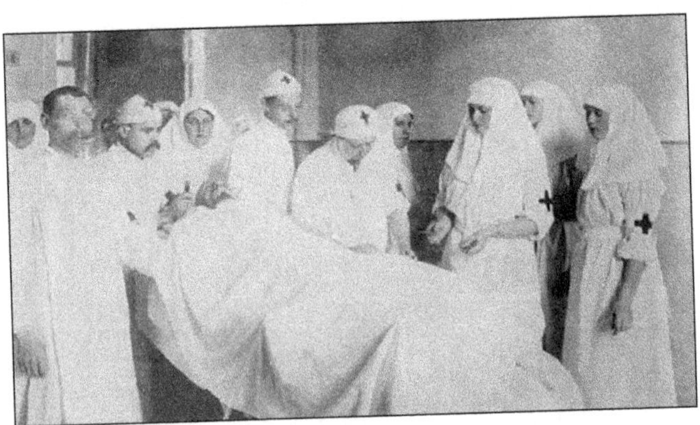

The Tsarina set the example of caring for others.
Here she is with her two oldest daughters.
(below left, and above)

In 1917, towards the end of her life, she wrote in her diary "In order to climb the great heavenly staircase of love, we must ourselves become a stone, a stair which others will climb." This quote takes my breath away! It is such incredible love for one's fellow man. I can see why Nicholas fell fast in love with Sunny — and not only for her physical beauty. When I look at the pictures I see a deep eternal love between them. She was his true love. Look for yourself and you will see it too! There was so much spiritual beauty there in that heart of hers!

As anyone can imagine, 26-year-old Nicholas was eager to marry his beautiful 22-year-old Sunny. When Nicholas's father, Tsar Alexander III, died just weeks before the wedding, the decision was made to wed before the official mourning period was over. The reason for this was they needed to get the coronation underway in order for the new Tsar Nicholas II to reign. The wedding took place at the Grand Church of the Winter Palace in Saint Petersburg, November 14/26; the newlyweds spent their honeymoon in mourning for Nicholas' father. The start of their life together makes me think about how Orthodox Christians refer to our life in this world as a *bright sadness* or a *joyful sorrow*. It is truly how they began their lives together.

The beautiful Tsarina in her wedding gown.

The year of their marriage was 1894. It was almost a brand new century. I remember learning as an art history major what was happening in European social circles and flooding into Russia at the time of their traditional Orthodox Christian marriage. Many well-known artists were openly discussing and practicing anti-Christian philosophies. Many strange and foreign beliefs like theosophy and spiritualism were becoming prevalent. It seems to me that lots of people were becoming ashamed of their faith and thought it was old-fashioned. They thought they knew more than God and began questioning the Godly traditional values, worship, and ways of living of their ancestors. God's commandments seemed primitive. People didn't want to be obedient; they wanted to explore new things.

Interestingly enough, it sounds like what's happening today in our world! Out with old ways and in with the new. As a consequence, many Europeans began to lose their true faith in God. Of course, we know this only eventually leads to disaster for any person or even a nation. But the future Tsar Nicholas II's wife would not have any of it. After accepting Chrismation she completely dove into Orthodox Christianity. She learned as much as she could about her adopted ancient Christian faith. She became completely devoted to it and saw Russian Orthodoxy as her identity. She became an example to others of what having a strong faith meant. My Mom used to tell me that a wife and mother is the beam that holds up the family home. I believe the future Empress was the "spiritual beam" that held her household together. She also served as a reality check for the people in her Imperial realm who were falling for the new spirit of the "Antichrist." The Empress was one of the holy pillars that held up Holy Imperial Russia by living out her great faith for all to see. We can see this in her photographs! Her virtuous life lives on in our hearts, and I believe she still continues to pray for Russia and the whole world, in heaven! She was always a caring Mother, or *Matushka*, for her beloved Russian people. This woman was a great follower of Christ and exemplified this towards her people through her charitable works and piety. Alexandra was not ashamed of her ancient Orthodox Christian Faith. She was wise. She knew there was no life without God.

Don't get me wrong; Nicholas had a great faith, too. That's what made them so compatible. Both of them not only loved God but also respected Him. They stood fast to holy tradition together. There is one part of an Orthodox Christian marriage that is my absolute favorite. It is called the Dance of Isaiah. I remember it fondly from my marriage. The bride and the groom process three times around a table on which the cross and the Gospel book are placed, a reminder that they must keep Christ at the center of the marriage. The hymns sung during this time are of blessing and martyrdom. The couple is set aside from the world to a union with Christ. Pondering their deep faith, I am always confused about the propaganda written about the Tsar and his beloved

Tsarina Alexandra. You always seem to read the same stuff: that she seemed haughty and cold. Or that he seemed aloof. But the people criticizing them do not see them in the right perspective. Everything they did revolved around God! In their marriage they were joined with Christ because He is the Bridegroom and the Church is His Bride. They agreed to be united together for life in His love. On the other hand, everything the contemporary world was doing around them was in the process of moving away from God. Sounds to me like nothing has changed in over 100 years! As Archimandrite Constantine of Jordanville has written, "Need one be amazed that the Tsar shut himself off? This was the chaste guarding of his spiritual personality from an alienated outer world."[8]

The future Tsar of Russia and his future Empress were a perfect match. They were crowned with honor and glory and both bore within themselves a deep Orthodox Christian faith. They were devoted servants of God. Nicholas chose his future wife wisely. He did so because the future Tsar of Russia, Nicholas II, was a wise and God-loving man.

+ + +

Chapter Three

GOD-ANNOINTED TSAR

"Blessed are the meek, for they shall inherit the earth."
Matthew 5:5 (KJV)

The official engagement picture of the Imperial couple.

God-Anointed Tsar

"Blessed are the meek, for they shall inherit the earth."

Their married lives would not be their own after the coronation. They were each about to embark on a difficult and demanding journey. They would have to be submissive and meek. They knew one day they would have to answer to God for their actions. I would call it a superhuman responsibility. A contract was about to be made; between God and his servant Nicholas, who was about to become the Emperor of Russia. He would serve God by fulfilling this contract. As Tsar he would, in turn, represent the Imperial coat of arms of the double-headed eagle, representing the ancient Byzantine harmony of Church and State. This coronation held in Uspensky Cathedral, Moscow, on May 26th, 1896, was to be the last one ever held in Russia.

The future Tsar wearing the Byzantine symbol of the double-headed eagle, signifying the harmony of church and state.

To really understand what it meant to become the Tsar of Russia, I turned to a surprise source — Nicholas' youngest sister, Olga. I realized that his youngest sister was to remain the last surviving member of the Romanov dynasty. She became the Imperial treasure that survived the Russian Revolution. Even better, not long before her death in 1960 her personal memoirs were compiled by her friend, Orthodox Christian author Ian Vorres. The result is an endearing book about her Imperial family called *The Last Grand Duchess*. I was so excited to find her book and realize I could read about her life! Olga had some impressive royal connections beyond her title of Grand Duchess. Both her father and brother share the title of Tsar! Imagine those roots for a moment. I love it because she shows us that her Tsar brother and Tsar father and their combined Imperial families were everyday people in ways we can relate to. Her special gift to us is to present a first-hand account of Imperial family life! There are so many revelations in her book that offer a true view into her beloved Imperial family as well as Russian Court life in general. Reading it is a delightful journey of discovery.

For example, Grand Duchess Olga states that she wished that her Tsar father had let her brother sit in on cabinet meetings. She points out that he was the heir, after all. But their father did not want state matters interfering with their happy family life. Only in 1893 did Nicholas sit in Council of State.[9] Olga shows us he basically had to learn how to be a Tsar "on the job." That could not have been easy for Nicholas because he was trained as a soldier but insufficiently as a statesman. However, he rose above this to his royal duty and with faith and courage made up for any traits he lacked in experience or training. In a word, he was relentless. I believe he became an incredible Tsar and did some amazing things.

His sister pretty much sums up the enormity of ruling as a Tsar better than anyone else. In fact, in her book she made a crystal clear statement about the traditional Orthodox Christian (non-Western) understanding of what being a God-anointed Tsar truly signified.

"It is all but forgotten today that to the Russian masses of my youth the Tsar was *chosen by God* to rule the country. Their devotion to him embraced their feelings for God and their country. Believe me; I have seen many examples of that truly dedicated affection. It was the main support of the Romanov sovereigns in their unrewarding task of wielding absolute power. Between the crown and the people was a relationship hardly ever understood in the West. That relationship had nothing to do with government or with petty officialdom. The Tsar and the people were bound together by the solemn vows of the Tsar's coronation oath when he pledged himself to rule, judge, and serve his people. In a Tsar the people and the office were joined together."[10]

Talk about spiritual! The coronation was a holy event! Most people may not even realize how holy a coronation really is. Nicholas — the newlywed — was about to embark on governing the largest nation in the entire world with his beloved consort Alexandra. He was not even 30 years old and he was to rule over one eighth of the entire world. Just thinking about it is enough to give me heart palpitations. I could not do it at any age! Talk about pressure. He was about to rule a nation that was a protector of the Orthodox Christian Faith.

Nicholas and Alexandra both prayed and kept to themselves prior to the big day. They were going to govern, but the governing was with God's help. That was clear to both of them. There was no turning back. It was their destiny by God's design, so they accepted it. They did not fight their destiny. You can see throughout the rest of their lives they took this seriously; the Tsar is and was, "Anointed by God." No one and no thing can ever change that, because this anointing is a sacrament or mystery in the Orthodox Church. This *mystery* is performed by the church during the coronation, and the Anointed of God (future Tsar) enters the Royal Doors into the altar, goes to the altar table and receives the Holy Mysteries as does the priest, with the Body and Blood taken separately. Thus the Holy Church emphasizes the great spiritual significance of the "podvig" (struggle) of ruling as a monarch, equaling this to the holy sacrament of the priesthood. It is no mere secular affair of state. Even the Tsar's future abdication on March 2, 1917 could not change who he had become during his coronation. So if you imagine him in heaven now — as I often do — he is still his Imperial Majesty, Tsar Nicholas II. He is now a Saint as well as a Tsar.

No one can ever take away the fact that he is and was a Tsar. The coronation had deep spiritual significance all the way around. Even sixty-four years after the event, the future Tsar's sister Grand Duchess Olga recalled that it ended with a very gentle and human climax, with the future Empress Alexandra kneeling before Nicholas. Olga never forgot how he carefully put the crown on Alexandra's head, how tenderly he kissed her, and how he helped her rise. As the coronation concluded, Grand Duchess Olga began to leave. She made a deep curtsey to Queen Victoria's representatives nearby, raised her head and saw her brother looking at her with such affection that her heart was all aglow. All those years later, she still remembered how passionately she vowed to dedicate herself to her country and her sovereign.[11]

Tsar Nicholas II on his coronation day.

Moscow was lit up that night with joyful celebratory fireworks following the coronation. Just when you thought it was time for the new Tsar and Tsarina to have some joy for themselves, a terrible black cloud descended. The general public had been invited to join in the planned celebration, and had been promised an Imperial gift. Imperial mugs filled with sweets were to be given out. They were to be distributed to all as souvenir gifts at a big field called Khodynka Meadow, just outside the city walls. About half a million people came, all waiting for their mugs. After that, there was to be an anticipated visit at noon from the Imperial couple. It's still a mystery as to what happened next. It's generally believed that there might have been a rumor spreading throughout the crowd that there were not enough mugs for everyone. Then somehow, a terrible stampede began for those mugs, which were set up on stands in the middle of the field. As you can imagine, death was everywhere on that field. The black cloud descended. I remember once — years ago — I had the chance to buy one of these actual souvenir Coronation cups. A Romanov memento would, I thought, be an amazing souvenir. It was even something I could afford. However, I just could not do it. The sadness of what happened that day kept staring back at me when I viewed that little Imperial mug.

Everyone was in mourning, and it was the start of propaganda against the new Imperial family. The Tsar and his wife spent the whole day visiting hospitals. They gave out pensions to the disabled, widows, and children of the tragedy. It is sad to think of this tragedy and the people who perished. It must have been a terrible way for the new Royals, who were no doubt devastated themselves, to start their new life and reign together. They began their accusations. The doors to propaganda against the Romanovs had been opened wide. And the new Tsar and Tsarina had to muddle their way through the horror together.

At least the new Tsar had a gentle wife by his side who lifted him up and gave him strength to bear the weight of his throne. She was his sunshine. I like to think of her as the Queen of piety and prayer. Tsar Nicholas' sister affectionately remembered that Empress Alexandra was absolutely wonderful to her brother the Tsar, especially in those first days when he was crushed by his manifold responsibilities. Her courage really saved him.[12]

Whenever I look at the photos, I see so much love between the two of them! Her love for him must have been his inspiration. Her meekness and faith must have been his peace. But to really understand the new Empress you have to always see her from a spiritual perspective. You have to open your eyes to a woman who had completely embraced her Russian Orthodox faith. Only then can you understand her actions, motives, and her life as a wife, Empress, and mother.

\+ + +

The two sides of this 1896 Russian Imperial Coronation Medal embody the Tsar-Martyr and Tsarina-Martyr's devotion to each other (above) and to the country they loved, served, and led in God's name (below).

Chapter Four

FAITHFUL FAMILY

"Blessed are those that hunger and thirst,
for righteousness, for they shall be satisfied."
Matthew 5:6 (KJV)

The Tsar and Tsarina leaving their coronation, embarking on their mutual journey of ruling one eighth of the world together.

Faithful Family

"Blessed are those that hunger and thirst for righteousness, for they shall be satisfied."

Joy was the cornerstone of their family life.

Photos reveal that Tsar Nicholas and his beloved Tsarina Alexandra, "Sunny" were a love match from the start. They remained deeply devoted to each other as their family began to grow. Their daughters came first: Grand Duchesses Olga, Tatiana, Maria and Anastasia. Their son and long-awaited Heir Tsarevich Aleksei was the youngest of their children.

Lovebirds.

The young Tsar and his Tsarina.

The stylish young couple.

Totally smitten.

The Tsar and Tsarina introducing their oldest daughter, Olga, to her great-grandmother Queen Victoria.

The doting mother with Anastasia.

Nicholas and Alexandra were both exceptionally loving and devoted parents. I love seeing the photos of the Tsar carrying his son around, or the tenderness evident in photos of Aleksei and his mother. Sometimes in photos you can see him playing with her signature necklace of pearls. Photos also show the girls respectfully gathered around their adored mother. They almost look like they are all waiting their turn for special time with her! Four girls makes one-on-one time with your mother precious. The more I learn about each of them, the more they appear to personify a loving and unified family that put God first in all things.

Theirs was an Orthodox Christian Monarchy, one that existed for the glorification of God and for the salvation of their people. Their family was the righteous role model for the entire Russian empire. As an Imperial family they were collectively pious and charitable in their activities. They worked out their salvation in front of everyone. Imagine that pressure! But from what I learn and see in the photos and home movies, they did it with grace, diligence, and devotion. They all seemed to be unique and different in their individual personalities. Viewed together as a family, they appear to be deeply bonded with one another. There is no question in my mind that they deeply loved each other. I feel so much of their love when I look at their photos. Sometimes the love I see overwhelms me. Their family life together had both joy and sorrow in equal measure. A real family they were — just like yours and mine in many ways.

You'd think the Imperial children would be spoiled, but they were not. I loved the description of the children's rooms and living conditions given by Anna Virubova. She emphasized that all the children had well-aired nurseries and slept on hard camp beds without pillows and with the least possible allowance of bed clothing. Their meals were plain, too. They had cold baths every morning and warm ones only at night. Yikes. I feel more spoiled than them! As a consequence, this simple life produced personalities that were unassuming and natural without a single trace of arrogance.[13] I also remember reading that their mother took charge of the smallest details in the educational upbringing of her daughters and only son. She prayed with them and was involved in each of their lives. She was especially interested in their religious instruction. It was said that the Empress alone trained Tsarevich Aleksei. She read to him daily from the Gospel and the lives of the Saints.

Tsarevich Aleksei was born with a rare illness called hemophilia, which is sometimes found in the bloodlines of Imperial families. When someone has hemophilia, their blood lacks certain proteins, so it won't clot normally. Any bump or bruise, even a minor one, could have potentially led to bleeding or even death for the heir to the throne. This illness was a heavy cross for him and the entire family to bear. I cannot imagine how I would even cope if he were my son. I think the Empress was much stronger than people realize. This and other tragedies in life offered ample ways for the

Imperial family to strive for spiritual crowns and rewards for their salvation. It seems to me that they bore so much pain in their lives. Seeing how they kept their eyes on God during their trials inspires me beyond words. They seemed to always navigate their lives with a deep faith in Gods supreme will paired with a great love for one another.

Aleksei, the youngest, bore his affliction of hemophilia with grace. Those who knew him said that suffering and self-denial left a long-lasting effect on his character. He could not play certain sports or do many of the things children his age could. This was very difficult for him because he was a child who loved the outdoors. Imagine him asking for a bicycle knowing he could not ride it. He was very sympathetic to the troubles and sicknesses of others as a result. He gave courtesy to his elders as well as to women and girls. He empathized with the Imperial servants when they had problems. Once he restored a young discharged servant to his position by hounding his father and giving him no rest until he did. The fruit of his illness gave rise to a unusually caring young fellow.[14]

The Tsarina cared very much about the children's characters. As her daughters matured it is said that she began to worry about their tendency towards superficial things, like frivolity and extravagance. The Empress also hated gossip. She tried to turn her girls' attention instead to the suffering of others in less fortunate circumstances. She got them involved in hospital work. This way she subdued any tendencies drawing them towards decadent social customs. She always tried to instill in them the fruits of the spirit.

Think of others first, then yourself. That's what I think the Empresses motto must have been raising her children. As a result, you will often see her daughters in photographs helping and ministering to suffering people. They put their nursing outfits on and went to work. That was a direct influence from their pious mother.

None of the beautiful spiritual examples the Empress expressed could change the minds of people who hated her. They were looking for things to use to slander her. She was fair game for lies and propaganda in the public courts. One of them still persists today and must be addressed. It's the rumor she had an intimacy with Russian peasant Grigori Rasputin and that he had an open door to the Russian Court and influence over the throne. All of this is untrue according to the Tsar's sister, Grand Duchess Olga. The only truth was that he had been to the palace a few times.

Before we get into this, try to imagine you had a child with this illness. Can you imagine what it would be like to have a child with hemophilia? I know I would be distraught. I would be desperate. I would give my life for my son. I know my health would be compromised due to my constant anxiety. Perhaps yours would be, too. What, then, would you do if two Orthodox Christian Bishops (Theofan and Hermogen) recommended you meet a wandering peasant, a so-called man of God [15] known to all who met him as a healer? Though he was never officially connected to the Orthodox Church, he had sinned and repented, and was a *strannik* (or pilgrim) who wandered from monastery to monastery. Even Saint John Kronstadt had been convinced by the sincerity of Rasputin's repentance.[16] Would you take the recommendation of a highly respected priest and two Bishops regarding his healing powers? Truth be told, I would try to meet him, too, if there was any chance at all that he could help my son.

In my opinion, the Tsar's sister Grand Duchess Olga writes the most convincing truth about Rasputin. She believed in his sincerity, but she did not like him or his thickly-slurred Siberian accent nor his primitive and uncouth ways. She said he was too curious in her presence — unbridled and embarrassing curiosity. The Grand Duchess continued that she found it difficult to understand why there were so few in Russia who believed that her nephew's terrible illness was the only reason for the Empress's trust and friendship with Rasputin. Faith in the power of prayer, in the gift of healing, and in miracles was common enough among the people. And Rasputin certainly possessed that gift of healing. "There is no doubt about it. I saw those miraculous effects with my own eyes and that more than once. I know the most prominent doctors of the day had to admit it. Professor Fedorov, who stood at the very peak of the profession and whose patient was Aleksei was, told me so on more than one occasion; and all the doctors disliked Rasputin intensely."[17] She went on to give examples of the many times Rasputin's prayers had the effect of healing upon Aleksei. Let's sift fact from fiction and lay the rumors about Rasputin the "Siberiak" (the man from Siberia) to rest. Most of all, let us have love and compassion for a mother who is anxious for her son's health. A mother who wants to save his life. Some may say I have a soft spot in my heart for the Empress, and as a mother, I would agree. Let us all put rumors aside, and put the spotlight back on the Tsarina-Martyr's beautiful heart.

Tsarina-Martyr Alexandra was a lot like her sister Elizabeth. Glittering society was not their cup of tea. They preferred the company of priests, monks, and nuns. In addition, they enjoyed being with their family and even simple peasant pilgrims. Church services and prayer took precedent over worldly interests. In photos and home movies you can even see the Empress kissing relics and crosses that masses of everyday Russian people had kissed.

My Serbian friend Mira Gacic-Spalatin went to visit the Tsarskoye Selo residence where the Imperial family used to live. I was thrilled when she brought me back a special gift. It was a packet of wonderful information and beautiful photographs of the living quarters of the Imperial family. I love studying the personal contents of each room. I read that many special gifts from a variety of people were treasured and displayed on their walls. Icons or holy images of God, the Mother of God or Saints were found in each of the children's rooms. It's important to remember that icons are not considered art or wall decoration per se. Icons are living theology. Orthodox Christians have them for use in personal prayer and to sanctify their homes.

The many icons we see in their home attest to the importance of the Imperial family's faith.

In Tsarevich Aleksei's room was the icon of Faith, Hope, and Love and their Mother Sophia. A Russian peasant woman gave it to him when he was born. The text written on the back was, "To glorify the birthday of our dear heir to the throne, Tsarevich and Grand Duke Aleksei Nicholaevich, given July 30, 1904 by a peasant woman who will pray to God and ask Him to give him all creature comforts and salvation and good health for many years to be, from a loyal subject of the monarchy — Nadezhda Shestakova from the village of Mazovka."[18]

It touched me to see that the Imperial family hung this icon in Tsarevich Aleksei's bedroom until 1917. That tells me how much the people of the Russian Empire loved the Tsar and his family, who truly treasured gifts from their subjects and found them meaningful. In Aleksei's room, for example, there were over 50 icons presented to him by sisters and relatives and loyal subjects. In the Tsarina's bedroom there were more than 700.[19] Over 700 icons in one room — imagine that! No doubt the number of her icons increased as the years went by. The poor Empress must have prayed constantly over the precarious health of her son. Her bedroom wall of icons gives us evidence of this. Faith was the backbone of everything in their lives. Their living spaces revealed what was important to this family. Theirs was an ongoing thirst for righteousness and a trust in the all-knowing providence of God. Even in their photos you could see God was the head of their home.

+ + +

Religious expression was an integral part of the Imperial family's everyday life and rule.

The entire Imperial family praying on their knees.

The Tsar praying and crossing himself.

The Tsarina's sister, Elizabeth, became an Orthodox monastic (nun) after her husband's death.

*The words "**All is in God's will**," found on the author's painting of Tsarina-Martyr Alexandra of Russia, are the first words of the Tsarina-Martyr's longer quote:*

> *"All is in God's will. The deeper you look, the more you understand that this is so. All sorrows are sent us to free us from our sins or as a test of our faith, an example to others. It requires good food to make plants grow properly and the gardener, walking through His garden, wants to be pleased with His flowers. If they do not grow properly, He takes His pruning knife, and cuts, waiting for the sunshine to coax them into growth again..."*

Chapter Five

GLORIFYING SAINT SERAPHIM OF SAROV

*"Blessed are the merciful,
for they shall obtain mercy."*
Matthew 5:7 (KJV)

Saint Seraphim of Sarov.

"...only the good deed done for Christ's sake brings us the fruits of the Holy Spirit. All that is not done for Christ's sake, even though it be good, brings neither reward in the future life nor the grace of God in this life. That is why our Lord Jesus Christ said: 'He who gathers not with Me scatters' (Luke 11 :23). "

Saint Seraphim of Sarov, 1754-1833

Glorifying Saint Seraphim of Sarov

"Blessed are the merciful, for they shall obtain mercy."

No matter what this good Imperial family did; the ugly rumors and propaganda persisted. In fact, it only grew! Of course, the enemies of God would not have liked knowing how many Churches were built during the Tsar's reign. More than 10,000! The same was true for monastery growth. Over 250 came to fruition! Pretty impressive, I think. You can see films of the emperor where he himself laid the first cornerstone for many new churches. He is also seen visiting churches and monasteries everywhere, all the while venerating their Saints. Christian literature and education flourished under his rule. In fact, there was no tsar in whose reign more Saints were glorified (canonized) than that of Tsar Nicholas II.[20]

The Tsar's love of his Russian Orthodox faith and its Saints seems boundless. Sometimes he even pressured the Holy Synod to speed up the glorification process of becoming a Saint.

The Tsar knew that Saints provided spiritual sustenance for his people and his Imperial family was also devoted to them. They even attended the glorification of a Saint that you may know, one who is among the most beloved and well-known Saints of the Orthodox Church. In my estimation, he is quite possibly the greatest Russian ascetic and wonderworker: Saint Seraphim of Sarov.

Icon of Tsar-Martyr Nicholas II holding Saint Seraphim of Sarov icon. Saint Seraphim was canonized in 1903 during the reign and prompting of Tsar Nicholas II.

Saint Seraphim would always try to inspire people to let the Holy Spirit into their hearts. This was his most famous quote: "Acquire the Spirit of Peace and a thousand souls around you will be saved." He would address people as, "my joy." He would keep silent and not judge anyone. Instead, he would love everyone. Now that he is a Saint — thanks to Tsar Nicholas II — we can all get to know him. Make his acquaintance and commune with him.

The Imperial family knew Saint Seraphim of Sarov and his reputation of sanctity. In fact, many of the Royal family members were healed by this Saint. Tsar Nicholas II repeatedly requested the Holy Synod of the Russian Orthodox Church to turn its attention towards Saint Seraphim's proposed glorification. It is said that the Tsar insisted upon the glorification but almost the entire Synod was against it. The only supporters were Metropolitan Anthony (Vadkovsky) and Archbishop Cyril (Smirnov).[21] Finally, in 1902, the petition for the elder's glorification was approved. One of my favorite photos of Tsar Nicholas II is when he is in procession with other men carrying the coffin and relics of Saint Seraphim during his 1903 glorification. Study and ponder that photo. That one little picture says so much about the Tsar.

Tsar Nicholas II, with members of his family, carrying the relics of Saint Seraphim of Sarov at the Saint's 1903 glorification.

The veneration and love the Imperial family had for Saint Seraphim was recorded many a time. One only has to do a little research and study their personal letters and diaries to come to this conclusion. It's obvious Empress Alexandra deeply loved Saint Seraphim and was also determined — like her husband — to see him made a Saint. After having four daughters she desperately wanted a son and heir. She had been praying to and asking for intercessory prayers from Saint Seraphim of Sarov for a son. So during the glorification festivities, the Empress went to Saint Seraphim's holy healing spring deep in the Sarov forest and immersed herself in the water, praying fervently for a son. There is a photo of her right after she came out of the holy spring. Only twelve months later her prayers were answered, and Tsarevich Aleksei was born. I loved to learn that Tsar Nicholas II had a large portrait of the future Saint mounted in his office. This gesture — his hanging Elder Seraphim's portrait in his office before the Saint's glorification — made a strong public statement, proclaiming to everyone the Tsar's belief in the sanctity of this future Saint long before his glorification was even approved.[22]

Tsarina Alexandra leaving the chapel over Saint Seraphim's healing spring in Diveyevo after bathing in the spring's waters. She immersed herself in the water, praying for a son. Twelve months later, Tsarevich Aleksei was born.

Saint Seraphim was also aware of the Tsar Nicholas II and Empress Alexandra from visions. He frequently spoke of this Imperial family during his lifetime — even though they were all to be born after his 1833 death. Saint Seraphim's spiritual son and historiographer was Nicholas Motovilov. He noted that in their discussions the Saint prophesied spiritual links to future Tsar Nicholas II and his Tsarina Alexandra. We have to remember this would have been before they were even born! He referred to the Tsarina Alexandra as devout. The Saint even said that the Tsar Nicholas II would have the soul of a Christian. In addition to predicting his own future glorification, he also said the Tsar would come to it with his family:

"The Tsar will come to us with his entire family. What joy there will be and Pascha will be sung in the summer."

Saint Seraphim's glorification was one of divine proportions. Part of the Tsar's duty as a God-appointed ruler was to see to it that the Church grew and remained healthy. Metropolitan Anthony of Saint Petersburg led the family and clergy in procession to the Cathedral of the Dormition. Holding the cross up, he then led the procession through the cathedral's west gate into the Church of Saints Zosima and Sabbatius. The elder's relics lay waiting there. After the coffin was censed, the crowd fell to their knees. Then Tsar Nicholas II and five grand dukes came forward. They lifted the coffin to their shoulders and carried it out from the church. They continued their procession into the town square while the crowd watched in silence, awe, and tears. Imagine being there. People scattered towels and scarves along their processional path so that they would have a holy memento from such a spiritually significant day.

As I imagine the moving scene in my head I keep wanting to say *thank you* to Tsar-Martyr Nicholas II and to Tsarina-Martyr Alexandra, who also pushed for the glorification. Together, they were such enthusiastic champions for Saint Seraphim's glorification! They are both responsible for giving us this wonderful Saint to venerate and learn from. They gave us the gift of this Saint to treasure — for the present and for all future generations. Saint Seraphim of Sarov is a true treasure! This humble Saint gives me hope to strive to love all people! Just to address someone as, "my joy," is to see the good in everyone because they are a creation of God. This Saint also gives us advice on how to practice an everyday prayer rule. He teaches that even the simplest of everyday prayers not only helps us reach Christian perfection, but also prepares us for our true future home, heaven! The earth is *not* our real home. Boy, do I need that reminder! Saint Seraphim also pushes me to focus in and work hard to live out the gospel, pray every day, and never lose my faith. He is *our* gift of hope and love — a gift everyone can be inspired by. The sermon given on the day of the glorification of this great Saint says it all:

"What message does the sepulcher hold for us? By the grace of God it is a heavenly reward for earthly righteousness, and the source of the most profound Christian feelings. We know that this coffin conceals the holy relics of a righteous one, a God-pleaser, a man of prayer and ascetic podvig, great in his simplicity, crowned with modesty and humility, burning with the love of Christ for everyone he met. In St. Seraphim's relics we come face to face with the profound truth of Holy Orthodoxy. In the relics of this man of prayer we sense the quickening life in our Russian Church. Our church is not dead, it has not grown cold or turned to stone; rather, adorned with new and righteous Saints it grows even younger and blossoms forth new shoots… These holy relics are a sign of the mercy and grace of God towards the Russian people and the Holy Orthodox Church. The heavens have opened to reveal a new man of prayer, a new intermediary and intercessor for us unworthy ones, who stand before the Lord for us… and in the tender joy of our faith, in the presence of the Saint in his wondrous icon, we sing to him: " We glorify thee, righteous Father Seraphim." Amen.

We have to always honor the holy memory of the righteous Saint Seraphim of Sarov. In addition, we must also begin to honor the Saints that glorified him. Saints that he spoke of before his death. We must forever be grateful that it was Tsar-Martyr Nicholas II who tirelessly pushed the petition forward for the holy elder's glorification. And again, let us not forget it was Tsarina-Martyr who also encouraged him to make this to happen.

They certainly made a good team to produce a future Saint who referred to the future Tsar before he was even born as being, "*most pious.*" and the future Tsarina as "*most devout.*" If you love Saint Serafim of Sarov, you cannot help but feel the same way about Tsar-Martyr Nicholas and the Tsarina-Martyr Alexandra and their holy family of Saints!

So, after so many years, these Holy Royal Martyrs are now proclaiming and revitalizing the Orthodox Christian faith around the world at this very moment. The church bells are ringing again in Russia. A far cry from Russia, at the Russian Orthodox monastery the Hermitage of the Holy Cross, in Wayne, West Virginia, there is a beautiful new Holy Shrine made to honor this family of Romanov Saints. It was designed by my good friend Andrew Gould, an American convert to Orthodoxy, and contains their relics. Their magnificent icons set within this shrine were painted in Russia by Natalia Aglitskaya and the carved stone icon inside the reliquary was made by another friend of mine, Jonathan Pageau. It may come as a surprise to some people that a great number of Americans have a pious devotion to these Russian Royal Saints. Now, we Americans don't necessarily have to make a pilgrimage to Russia to be with them! They are now available for everyone, no matter where we live. Saints that continue to build God's Kingdom even now — from heaven. Think about that.

This American Shrine designed by Andrew Gould is dedicated to the Holy Royal Martyrs of Russia. It is located at the Hermitage of the Holy Cross, a Russian Orthodox monastery located in Wayne, West Virginia.

Ariane with her remarkable friend, Andrew Gould, one of the New World Byzantine designers whose website can be found at www.newworldbyzantine.com. It was Andrew who designed the magnificent Holy Royal Martyr Shrine on the previous page, which was installed just in time to commemorate the centenary of their martyrdom.

In each of our lives, it is wonderful to know the Holy Royal Martyrs can now intercede for us. They hear us. Talk to them. They will guide you from darkness and confusion to the light of God. Even the Tsarina-Martyr herself ended a letter to an officer once by saying: "My soul will be always be near, and will always and everywhere follow you and protect you from every evil with prayers."[23] These letters have now been translated and are ready to be published in English by the Holy Transfiguration Monastery in Brookline, Mass. The translation of the two letters presented here was made by Natalia Challis. The Tsarina's words are a prophetic example of a Saint's words. Sometimes when I go about my day I say: *Holy Martyrs, pray to God for me*! You can too. We can ask the Royal Martyrs to pray to God to have mercy on us. The simple truth is we need to remember them in our prayer life. We may have lost them here on earth, but they are very much alive in heaven. Commune with them. They will hear you and pray for you. Once you get to know these Saints they become truly unforgettable in your life!

\+ + +

The Simple Rule

OF ST. SERAPHIM OF SAROV:

Let any Christian, upon arising from sleep stand before the holy icons, and read the Lord's Prayer "Our Father" thrice, in honor of the Most-holy Trinity, then the hymn to the Theotokos "O Theotokos and Virgin, rejoice..." three times as well, and finally, the Symbol of Our Faith once. Having completed this rule, let each one attend to the tasks to which he was appointed or to which he is called.

During work at home or while traveling somewhere, let him quietly read "Lord Jesus Christ, Son of God, have mercy on me a sinner." If there are others in his vicinity while he is working, let him silently repeat "Lord have mercy," until supper.

After supper, upon completing his tasks, let him quietly read "Most Holy Theotokos, save me a sinner," and let him repeat this until falling asleep.

Going to bed, let any Christian again read the above-mentioned morning rule. Thereafter, let him go to sleep, having protected himself with the sign of the Cross." Fr. Seraphim said "Keeping this rule, it is possible, to reach Christian perfection, for the three prayers indicated are the foundation of Christianity.

THE LORD'S PRAYER

Our Father, Who art in the heavens, hallowed be Thy name. Thy kingdom come, Thy will be done, on earth as it is in heaven. Give us this day our daily bread, and for give us our debts, as we forgive our debtors; and lead us not into temptation, but deliver us from the evil one.

Hymn to the Most-Holy Theotokos

O Theotokos and Virgin, rejoice, Mary full of grace, the Lord is with Thee; blessed art thou among women, and blessed is the Fruit of thy womb, for thou hast borne the Savior of our souls.

The Symbol of our Faith

I believe in one God, the Father Almighty, Maker of heaven and earth, and of all things visible and invisible.

And in one Lord Jesus Christ, the Son of God, the Only-begotten, begotten of the Father before all ages;

Light of Light; true God of true God; begotten, not made; of one essence with the Father; by Whom all things were made; Who for us men, and for our salvation, came down from the heavens, and was incarnate of the Holy Spirit and the Virgin Mary, and became man; And was crucified for us under Pontius Pilate, and suffered and was buried; And arose again on the third day according to the Scriptures; And ascended into the heavens, and sitteth at the right hand of the Father; And shall come again, with glory, to judge both the living and the dead; Whose kingdom shall have no end. And in the Holy Spirit, the Lord, the Giver of life;

Who proceedeth from the Father; Who with the Father and the Son together is worshipped and glorified; Who spake by the prophets. In One Holy Catholic and Apostolic Church. I confess one baptism for the remission of sins. I look for the resurrection of the dead, and the life of the age to come. Amen.

Chapter Six

HOLY ROYAL CHILDREN

"Blessed are the pure in heart,
for they shall see God

Matthew 5:8 (KJV)

While working on this chapter, the author was inspired to begin painting the Holy Royal-Martyr Innocents, portrayed here left to right: Maria, Tatiana, Anastasia, Olga, and Aleksei.

Holy Royal Children

"Blessed are the pure in heart, for they shall see God."

I remember the day over a decade ago when I met author and fellow Orthodox Christian, Christine Benagh. Somehow her book came into my possession. It is called *An Englishman in the Court of the Tsar.* She wrote this historic book documenting the life and times of Englishman, Charles Sydney Gibbes. He was one of three tutors to the Imperial Romanov children. The Tsarina-Martyr herself summoned him to be a royal tutor. As a result, he gained entrance to the inner world of the Imperial Russian family. The author traveled to England and met the family of this Romanov tutor. She had cultivated a connection to the inner circle of the Imperial family. In the course of reading her wonderful book I realized she lived in Nashville. My heart nearly stopped. I exclaimed to myself, we live in the same city! I had to meet her. A woman who loved history and especially the last Russian Royal Family. I felt we were destined to meet — and we did. In fact, she gave me my very first two icons of the Holy Royal Martyrs Nicholas and Alexandra which I keep by my bedside. She has since passed away so this chapter is for you, Christine. Memory Eternal, my friend.

We made an agreement to meet and chat once a month for almost a year. I learned so much from this beautiful lady. Her book will also help you to understand world history at the time of Tsar Nicholas II. Christine lived in a small apartment with many icons by her front door. She was elderly by the time I met her, but still sharp as a tack and excited and eager to discuss the Romanov Martyrs with me. She loved the Royal family. We were compatible from the moment we met. It was almost like I was speaking to an older version of myself. She knew history like nobody's business. She topped me on that! But of all our history talks, it always came back to the subject of our faith. This was always the starting point in any discussion we had. She wanted me to understand this family through our mutual faith. Christine kept repeating to me that this Englishman was spiritually transformed throughout the years by this Royal family. He witnessed firsthand the deep and profound faith expressed not only by the parents, but also by their children. This vigorous Christian faith was firmly instilled in the Royal children from the start.

Christine told me the Tsarina asked Gibbes to teach Anastasia first. "She was eight years old at the time. It was 1909, and it was the first time Gibbes met the Tsarina. He said she still looked very young with beautiful hair, eyes, and complexion. She gave you her hand with dignity mingled with shyness, which truly gave her a gracious air, very pleasurable to see and feel. He went on to describe little Anastasia as a lady of great self-possession, always bright and happy. Ever bent on inventing some new oddity of speech or manner, her perfect command of her features was remarkable. I have never seen anything quite equal to it in any other child."[24]

Christine always stressed that from all her research on the family, that they were a tightly knit family whose love for each other was genuine. She said Gibbes noted that the children had to adjust their classroom schedules for the midmorning walk which the children took regularly with their Tsar father when the weather and his schedule permitted. Then Gibbes observed the family's overall devotion to their faith and their great love for God. Additional schedule adjustments in their coursework — like those that must have been made for their midmorning walk — assured that time was also made for all the church services the family unfailingly attended throughout the course of the year. Orthodoxy had deep roots in Russia, and the Imperial family faithfully continued this long held tradition, belief and submission to an All-Mighty and Powerful God.

I loved reading the honest impressions that this English-born tutor had of Russia. Christine told me in our discussions that Russia remained culturally Christian more that any Western nation. So, Gibbes was experiencing a country that still strongly maintained a nearly thousand–year-old heritage of Orthodox Christianity. This was all new to him. By comparison, the England he came from was quite secular in appearance. He was especially struck by all the icons in Russia. I wonder what he first thought of them. They were a sight he would not have seen prevalent in England. However, in Russia he noticed they were everywhere! He saw these visual reminders of the presence of God and His glory in shops, on coaches and sleds, and over doorways and bridges. Even the outside of churches had them. Russian houses all had their, "Krasnyi ugol," a "bright" or "beautiful corner." All of this must have been a lot to absorb for Nicholas Gibbes. Melodious pealing of many-toned bells from hundreds of churches and monasteries calling the faithful to worship must have struck him in some deep way. The radiant golden domes of churches filled his sight.

Everywhere he looked were reminders of heavenly realms. Whether you were Royal or peasant, if you were Orthodox you could participate through the sacred mysteries (sacraments). The ancient Christian rites and ceremonies were deeply woven into the daily routine of this devout family. It was not fake. It was not put on. The Imperial Romanov family piety was the cornerstone of their happiness and mutual affection. He could not miss seeing all this with his own eyes. Neither could he avoid being thoroughly exposed to the ancient Russian Orthodox faith through his work with the Royal children. Christine told me that it was through the direct exposure and influence of this family of faith that Gibbes, himself, converted and eventually became the first English Orthodox Abbott in history! Imagine that: He started out as young royal tutor and ended his life as a monastic priest!

The key that opened this Englishman's mind to choosing a faith so foreign to his background had to have been inspired by his close contact with these dear children. You can see from the photographs that they were all quite beautiful. It was the hearts of these children that had to have precipitated a change in Mr. Gibbes. He worked with the children and came to possess a deep familiarity with them. Almost like family, I would think. This special time with them was to eventually bring about a spiritual transformation in him later in life.

My friend Christine would have loved a beautiful article I just recently discovered on the children. It touches upon many of the things she told me Mr. Gibbes had observed about them. It is beautifully written with love by Matushka Natalia Sheniloff. I think it's important to hear descriptions of the children from someone who shares the same faith.

Matushka starts by describing Olga, the oldest, who was born in 1895. She was fair, with golden-brown hair (the lightest in the family) and beautiful blue eyes. She was innocent, modest, sincere, and kind. She was most similar to her father, whom she loved better than anyone else. She had a quick mind and possessed the virtue of reasoning. According to her tutors, she had a "crystal" soul and a bright smile; inner joy radiated from her and had an uplifting effect on those around her. Like her father, Olga deeply loved Russia and the Russian people. When faced with the possibility of marriage to a foreign prince, she flatly refused saying, "I do not want to ever leave Russia. I am Russian and wish to remain so." Thus she stayed on in her homeland to receive the crown of martyrdom.[25]

Olga

The next daughter, born in 1897, was named Tatiana. Such a beautiful name! I considered naming my daughter Tatiana, which was on our short list, but the name Ana won out! Tatiana is still close to my heart. What a beautiful name for a gorgeous child who was her mother's favorite. Tatiana inherited the Tsarina's sense of discipline, leadership, and nobleness. She was darker in complexion than the other children. She was dutiful and pensive. The younger children called her "the Governess." Tatiana was also artistic. She painted, embroidered, and was a talented pianist.

Tatiana sitting with her sister, Anastasia.
Tatiana is holding her dog Ortino.

Tatiana

The third child, another daughter, was named Maria. She was born in 1899. I look at her photos and her eyes speak to me the most. They draw me in somehow. There is a friendly liveliness to them. Maria loved children. It's easy to imagine that she would have been an excellent mother. She was also artistic. One of her lovely qualities was to be happy at any given circumstance. Maybe it's a middle child trait. Either way she made the best of things even in the worst of times. That's a quality I wish I had.

Maria

The fourth and youngest daughter was Anastasia. She was born in a new century, 1901. She had beautiful gray eyes, and she was known as the family clown. She loved to make everyone laugh. God knew what he was doing when he created her. The family needed this little joy of a girl! She was artistic, kind, and loved animals. She had a small doggie that the whole family adored, that she carried down into the cellar that terrible night the Bolsheviks murdered the entire family.

Anastasia

The youngest child was the long-awaited Tsarevitch Aleksei, the heir apparent. This was the child that Tsarina had prayed for as she dipped herself in Saint Seraphim of Sarov's spring. I remember reading in the article by Matushka Natalia that: *he was destined for martyrdom from the moment of his birth.* As much as I don't want to look at it this way, she is correct. She compares him to young Isaac in the Old Testament. Aleksei was an innocent, a sacrificial lamb who was sacrificed to atone for the sins of his people. It was discovered that he had hemophilia when he was only six weeks old, and he bore the illness as a true Christian. Christine mentioned he would cross himself constantly and say the Jesus Prayer during his painful bleeding episodes. ("Lord Jesus Christ, Son of God, have Mercy on me, a sinner.") I have a son and believe living with hemophilia would have been a living martyrdom for him and for his entire family. Aleksei must have wanted to be a normal boy and not different due to his illness. He would have wanted to have fun and do outdoor activities and go sailing with his father. And yet, people who knew him said he was clever and kind and loved animals. He was a cheerful and lively child who loved to give people gifts. Everyone who met him loved him. When you look at his photos he looks so happy. I really see the joy. I also see the deep loving bond he had with his mother the Tsarina. My author friend Christine repeatedly told me that Mr. Gibbes referred to Tsarevitch Aleksei as, "The beautiful child." I can see why. Spiritual beauty makes physical beauty even more blindingly radiant.

Aleksei with his mother.

Alexis
1914

Think of poor dear Tsarina. Imagine her grief knowing that the cruel illness he bore his whole life was inherited from her side of the family. I feel her pain just thinking about it. I hope in time we have more Orthodox Churches and Monasteries here in the United States and abroad named in honor of this beautiful family of Royal Martyrs. Not only can we learn from the parents but also from the children who are holy examples for us.

The Tsar and Tsarina gave their children a perfectly glorious Orthodox Christian upbringing. They knew the order of life: God first in all things. It was clear all of them were innocent and pure. They were pious. As Matushka Natalia points out regarding the Royal Martyrs: Their Calvary began on March 2, 1917, the day of the Tsar-Martyr's abdication — first in their palace at Tsarskoye Selo, then at the Governor's house in Tobolsk, and ended, finally, at Ipatiev house — the "House of Special Purpose"— in Ekatererinburg. They suffered increasing stages of harassment, humiliation, and deprivation. Their prison guards became progressively more insolent, heartless, and brutal, subjecting them to insult, mockery, and torment. The royal martyrs bore it all with great fortitude, strength of spirit, true Christian humility, and total acceptance of the will of God. They sought solace in church services, home prayers, and spiritual reading. They were heinously murdered, these pure and innocent children, on the night of July 4/17, 1918 and from the blood-soaked cellar in Ekaterinburg, they passed triumphantly into the royal palace of the King of Heaven.[26]

A guileless and loving family, the Holy Royal Martyrs loved God first and being with each other second.

Chapter Seven

APOSTLE OF PEACE

"Blessed are the Peacemakers,
for they shall be called the sons of God."
Matthew 5:9 (KJV)

17600 **PROPOSITION DE NICOLAS II.**

D'ordre de l'empereur, le comte Mouraview a remis, le 24 août, à tous les représentants étrangers accrédités à St-Pétersbourg, la communication suivante :

Le maintien de la paix générale et une réduction possible des armements excessifs qui pèsent sur toutes les nations se présentent dans la situation actuelle du monde entier comme l'idéal auquel devraient tendre tous les efforts de tous les gouvernements.

Les vues humanitaires et magnanimes de Sa Majesté l'empereur, mon Auguste maître, y sont entièrement acquises, dans la conviction que ce but élevé répond aux intérêts les plus essentiels et aux vœux légitimes de toutes les puissances ; le gouvernement impérial croit que le moment présent serait très favorable à la recherche, dans la voie de la discussion internationale, des moyens les plus efficaces à assurer à tous les peuples les bienfaits d'une paix réelle et durable, et à mettre avant tout un terme au développement progressif des armements actuels.

Tsar Nicholas II's invitation to representatives of other governments, to join him at The Hague, Netherlands, for an international conference on peace and disarmament. The invitation was issued on 24 August 1898, with the conference beginning on the Tsar's birthday, 18 May 1899 (O.S. 6 May).

Apostle of Peace

"Blessed are the Peacemakers,
for they shall be called the sons of God."

Our great God The King of Heaven is also known as the Prince of Peace. "His Name will be called wonderful, mighty God, everlasting Father, Prince of Peace. Of the Increase of His government and the peace their will be no end." (Isaiah 9:6-7) Tsar Nicholas II began his rule early on exemplifying one of God's extraordinary precepts. It was the principle of peace. One of the first major acts of his reign revolved around this principle. It must have come easily to him due to his devout faith and guileless nature. Additionally, the Tsar was well-versed in history. He understood the evils of war. The violence and tragedy of war was experienced and understood by all countries. Much time and money have been spent acquiring weapons of mass destruction. Wars have brought untold suffering, ruined cities, and uprooted families in every nation. My own family was uprooted from the former Yugoslavia. Wise Tsar Nicholas II saw the big picture. He approached his ruling throne as the Christian that he was and became the first world leader to come up with an idea to invite governments of all major nations to join an international peace conference for the discussion of formal limitations of armaments.

Can you imagine such a proposition back then? Forget the weapons, he said, let's talk about peace! He was living out a teaching of the Gospel. The Christ-like Tsar knew the Gospel. He knew God's way is the best and *only* way. He knew that hostile divided governments would end up nowhere. However, if leaders met in person and respectfully conversed with each other, perhaps real progress could be made. There would be hope for peace and maybe even more prosperity for all. So, by the initiative of Tsar Nicholas II, this peace conference convened at The Hague in 1899.

At first, his idea was met with skepticism and disbelief. However, as soon as the United States agreed to jump on the peace conference bandwagon, all other nations followed suit. It was a historic conference. The Tsar's peace conference laid the groundwork for the League of Nations and the future United Nations. Many people do not realize the Tsar was the driving force behind this initiative. This was entirely his idea. Again, this tells you about the Tsar's great and noble heart. He was truly an "Apostle of Peace."

I think that people who dislike the Tsar will continue to, no matter what is said. However, those who have ears to hear, let them hear; and those who have eyes to see, let them see. This Tsar was an incredibly merciful Tsar. He pardoned even the worst of criminals — even revolutionaries that wanted to kill him! He also gave away much of his money and land to help the peasants. He knew they were his beloved Russian people![27] It is believed that he gave away the last of his wealth during World War I. As a young fellow, he spent his allowance to help poor students pay for their tuition. He wanted people to have a better life. He changed an old passport system introduced by Peter I so people could travel, especially abroad. He eliminated a poll tax and introduced a generous hospital insurance for his people. In 1897, the Tsar enacted a law to limit work hours for women and minors; night work was forbidden — unlike the majority of countries in the West. That's pretty modern for its time: Labor legislation. The Tsar sincerely cared about his Russian people. I love watching vintage movies of the Tsar on his knees blessing his troops. I see him so engaged and deeply interested in his Russian people. He was devoted to his duty as Emperor. It wasn't just for show. You can tell when you observe his face. He cared. He loved his people as a good father does.

There is so much the West does not understand about the Tsar. Even today this still holds true. For example, a constitutional monarch like the one we see in England fulfills the will of the people, and can be ignored or deposed by them as they see fit. Remember Edward VIII and his abdication. He did it to please himself and to live a life of pleasure of his own choice. He was basically unfit to rule. He did not care about respecting his Church or his faith. At the end of his life he reflected, "What a wasted life!"[28]

As God-anointed Tsar, Nicholas II was an Orthodox Christian autocrat. That means he had to uphold the Orthodox Faith. Study history. You won't find one story where he goes against his faith. Not one. He always set his ego aside for the greater good of his great Lord and his people. He did not want to abdicate. However, without getting into details, there was no fighting back on his part regarding his abdication. After an entire night in prayer, he sadly determined that if it could help avoid bloodshed and if it was for the good of his country, he would not fight back. He submissively laid aside his crown and accepted his fate. The terrible part was that the majority of Russians loved him and did not want him to abdicate. He was being fed lies from the enemies of God. He even said at one point he felt lies and deceit all around him. During this terrible time he wrote these lines which illustrate his deep love for his Russian people and their salvation:

"I am ready to give up both throne and life if I should become a hindrance to the happiness of the homeland. There is no sacrifice that I would not make for the real benefit of Russia and for her salvation."

We all know that feeling when something just feels off — like a black cloud. Little by little, evil was surrounding the Tsar. They had a name: Bolsheviks. They also had a leader, Lenin. No matter what happened during this bleak and depressing time, we must remember one simple point. The Tsar's abdication really meant nothing since the power of an anointed Tsar is from God. No one can ever take that away. Once a Tsar, always a Tsar.

The God-ordained Tsar Nicholas II and his legacy, Aleksei.

The terrible truth was that Lenin and his puppets were moving in and encircling Holy Russia and the God-loving Tsar and his virtuous family. I have a hard time looking at some of the photos from 1917-1918. The sadness is tangible and real. The Tsar sitting on the tree stump right after he abdicates with those harsh guards behind him. His gentleness speaks volumes. I cannot even bear to look at this photo for too long because my heart really hurts. The Tsar's face says so much. He is still the God-loving Tsar. The way he sits and comports himself is inherently kind, humble, and noble. But the sadness is too much to bear. Lenin, who orchestrated the terrible fate of our Saints and their eventual martyrdom, was the exact opposite of them: a fierce enemy of our Lord God. Lenin's aim was to achieve a worldwide god-like status as leader of his Bolshevik and later renamed Communist Party.

Believe it or not, Lenin was a hereditary nobleman. He was a professional revolutionary who lived on party funds and income from his mother's estate. He never worked like you or me. He lived underground so he had no idea how regular people lived, worked, or suffered. In fact he had a contempt of ordinary people — Russian or not. Once he said, "I spit on Russia." His actions and words showed contempt for Russians of all classes. Once I read all the disparaging and downright evil obscenities Lenin enjoyed calling the Russians, and it literally made me sick. I cannot even write the words he said here. The real truth is that Lenin's revolution was not carried out to help everyday, hard-working Russians. It was not carried out for the love of anybody or anything, but simply out of irrational, demonic, universal hatred.[29]

The Yugoslavian Communist regime my parents fled from in the 1950s was an atheistic one. I remember them often discussing the evils of Communism. Orthodox Christian writer Vladimir Moss says if we study Communist history we will find that the Communists' extraordinary hatred of God and Christians, and indeed mankind in general, can only be explained by demon-possession — more precisely, by an unconscious compulsion to bring blood-sacrifices to the devil, who was, in Christ's words, "a murderer from the beginning." (John 8:44)[30] I remember writing an essay in middle school on Chinese Communist leader Mao Tse-Tung (now commonly spelled Mao Zedong), whose ideas seemed to me even then to be cold, egotistical, and anti-Christian, and now we know his economic and social campaign killed forty-five million people between 1958 and 1962. Communism is evil. Anything without God has no goodness.

The Russian Monarchy must have really bothered the demonic Lenin. The Russian Army recovered after some losses and was becoming successful and even confident. Russia was on its way to becoming one of the most powerful and prosperous countries in Europe. It entered the First World War with the largest army in the world. Imagine the threat to satan if Russia won the war! Lenin had to act and he did. Confusion began to swirl around the Tsar, who was being vilified in the press. He was given false information on purpose and his commands were being ignored. His top generals were begging him to abdicate. When the Tsar answered them all and said, "There is no such sacrifice which I would not make for the benefit of Russia," these were the words of a Godly man. Lenin would never have put others first and said such words. On the day of his abdication, the Tsar wrote in his diary, "All around me is treason, cowardice, and deceit." He must have felt the Holy Spirit warning him of the evil surrounding him. Tsar Nicholas II's abdication of the throne took place on 2/15 March, 1917.

Kindred souls, the Tsar and his devoted personal physician, Evgeni Botkin (who was also later recognized as a Saint), remained duty-bound to fulfill the roles God had given them, and stayed together until their tragic deaths.

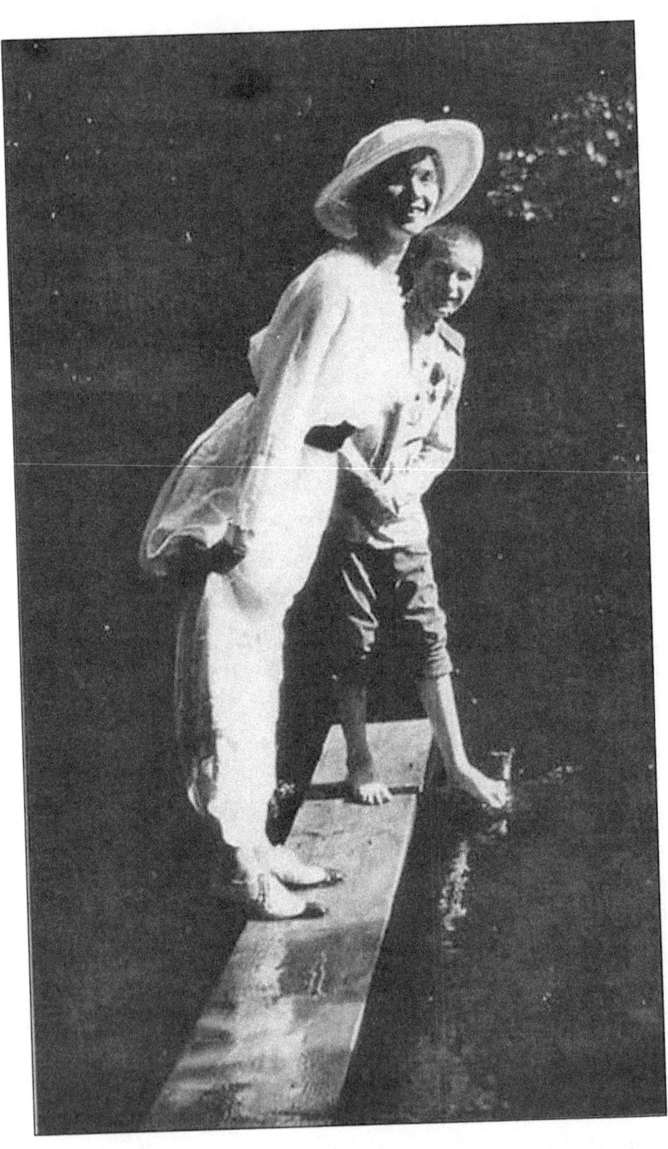

Innocence and joy were embodied by siblings Olga and Aleksei — even here on the day before their family's imprisonment, which preceded their eventual martyrdom.

The Tsar's abdication day marked the beginning of terrible sufferings for millions of Russian people. It was followed by the new and awful era of an anti-God criminal regime. This Orthodox Christian Tsar had been a *formidable obstacle* to the Antichrist to come. People should have been kissing his feet and thanking him. But in our human stupidity we kicked him out. Now the road was free and clear for the dread Antichrist. God help us all!

\+ + +

The "Reigning" (Derjavnaja) Icon of the Mother of God revealed itself to the Russian Orthodox people on the exact day of Tsar-Martyr Nicholas II's abdication, 2/15 March 1017, in the village of Kolomenskoe, near Moscow.

Chapter Eight

AN ICON AND A VISION

"Blessed are those that are persecuted,
for righteousness sake,
for theirs is the kingdom of heaven."
Matthew 5:10 (KJV)

The author's portrait of Tsar-Martyr Nicholas II.

An Icon and a Vision

"Blessed are those that are persecuted for righteousness sake, for theirs is the kingdom of heaven."

Tsar Nicholas II loved our Lord God and his Most Pure Mother and his Russian people. Photographs of him pictured alone speak volumes at different periods of his life. I have studied the photos of him taken around the time of his March 1917, abdication. I see such tremendous sorrow in his eyes, and they continue to draw me in. Lenin's eyes repel. They are cold and steel-like in any photo I see of him. I see other photos of Lenin screaming with maniacal force. I see no peace in him. I do see an inherent peace in the Tsar, even in sorrow. We know the old saying, "the eyes are the windows of the soul." These two men are perfect examples of polar opposites. One man was for God and is now a Saint; the other one was against God and has been condemned by history. It is obvious in more ways than one. I know I am an artist and so maybe I am more visually sensitive than some. There is one thing

I do know for sure. The more you take time to look and study these old photos, the more you will see. Look and see for yourself. Don't just rely on some secular documentary that tells you a general history of Russia and its Tsars. Remember: not all Tsars are Saints. God allowed these photographs of the Holy Royal Martyrs to give evidence to the *Truth*.

Tsar Nicholas II and Lenin:
The juxtaposition of good versus evil.

Do we have eyes to see? Look at a photo of Lenin. One doesn't need to read a volume to see that those are not eyes that draw the viewer in. Those are eyes that *repel*. Scary, contemptful eyes. Evil eyes. I bet you, too, can see this. It just takes a moment to study them. I see eyes insensitive to the sufferings of others. I can relate to how the insightful scholar Vladimir Moss describes the cult of Lenin. He basically says that Lenin saw himself as nothing less than a Messiah, not just for Russia but for the entire world. He goes on to say that his party and his teaching reflected that of *the psychology of the Antichrist*. He had no morals and his mindset was that of a criminal. What really sickens me is that he took special pleasure in news of murders, both individual and still more mass murders, carried out with impunity. At such moments he was sincerely happy. This bloodthirstiness is the key to that special power that "the leader of the world proletariat" received from the devil and the angels of the abyss. People don't realize how his teaching conquered millions of minds in Russia. This is the answer: Leninism is a religion, a cult of personality, from Lenin to Stalin and so on. Each successive leader was nourished by demonic forces. Lenin formed the religion of the coming Antichrist. The faithful Leninist, Stalin, had his corpse embalmed and kept on display for the masses to see — the cult of Lenin.

Tsar Nicholas II and his family left behind a beautiful trail of photos for everyone to see. Like Christ, the Tsar suffered for his people. He bore the weight of the cross and carried it until the end. But even in these horrific times, God was with him and his beloved Russian people. The light of heaven was still streaming in through dark foreboding clouds during the time of his abdication, just as the Bolshevik Revolution led by Lenin moved quickly to remove anything related to God.

In the midst of that time, God allowed a miracle in the form of a little girl and an icon. Not many people know the story.

You may remember that icons are painted for veneration and prayer. These representations of a transfigured spiritual reality of God and His Saints remind us not only to pray to our Lord but to remember Him. Let's be honest; it is easy to forget God. My icons of particular Saints are my windows to heaven. Seeing icons in my home or at church are my continual reminder not to forget God.

Even during tragic times, icons of God and His Saints prompt us to remember Him so that His will can take over. I don't know what I would do without my icons. They prompt me to pray and even talk to God and the Saints when life is going well *and* when I need help. They are physical, three-dimensional matter, but they point us to our true heavenly home which is invisible to us here. I am glad I have them to remind me of our Great Lord God, who never forgets us. He always loves us.

That's why I adore this story. I think it's best told by an amazing scholar of art history and the theology of the icon, Irina Yazykova. Irina wrote a book that anyone who loves icons should get, called *Hidden and Triumphant*. Her book is about the underground struggle to save Russian Iconography. I encourage you to read this historic book. I am not an iconographer, but I took several classes with Russian iconographer Ksenia Pokrovsky. She is featured in a section of this wonderful book. Ksenia was one of the brave heroes who continued to paint holy images secretly during the God-less Soviet Union. She also helped preserve the ancient

Byzantine tradition of Iconography painting by teaching it to a new generation.

The Revolution was worse than we can even imagine. It precipitated the systematic closing and destruction of churches. As if that wasn't enough, they imprisoned, tortured, and killed clergy. The destruction of holy images of God went along with all of this horror. God was out and in turn, icons had to go. What's really sad is that all these beautiful icons were carted up, burned, and destroyed by Russians themselves. These were baptized Christians who fell for all the Bolshevik propaganda. They fell under the influence of satan, the great destroyer. I even found old pictures with children giving their icons to be destroyed. I cannot bear to look at any of these pictures. They say a lot about the hearts of the people back then. The revolutionaries brainwashed them to think God was not necessary. It's as if they wanted to throw God away! It makes you weep. However, you cannot destroy the Great Builder, our Lord God. Sometimes in order to build, you have to break things down first. God in his great mercy still chose to reveal a miraculous icon to the Russian people during this terrible time.

So, back to our story of the special icon and a little Russian village girl. The discovery of this icon on March 2/15, 1917 (Tsar Nicholas II's abdication day), and the miraculous timing of its appearance, coincides exactly with the terrible revolutionary upheavals that were happening. This is what the author, Irina, writes about the appearance of this icon of the Mother of God:

"The very day of the emperor's abdication, a peasant girl named Evdokia Adrianova, who lived in the village of Pererva outside of Moscow, was given a vision in a dream. She saw Mary, the Mother of God, who told her to go to the village of Kolomenskoe and find there an old icon, which, Mary told the girl, "will change color from black to red." The peasant girl was uneducated but pious and didn't dare disobey.

"When she arrived in the village of Kolomenskoe she described her vision to a priest in the Church of the Lord's Ascension. The priest took her at her word and helped her search for the icon. He went through the church and all the adjoining buildings until finally, in a storage room filled with odds and ends, he found a large, old icon left there because of its dilapidated condition. The icon was so blackened that one could barely make out the contours of a throne on which the Mother of God was seated with the Holy infant in her lap.

"When they took the icon out into the light, however, before their very eyes the blackness began to fade, and the image became more and more clear. The Mother of God's clothes gradually turned a color as red as blood; the crowns on both Mary's and Christ's heads became visible, and in Mary's hands appeared a scepter and orb — signs of monarchical authority. As the Mother of God had predicted, the icon did "change color from black to red."

Since this took place on the same day as the emperor's abdication of the throne, the appearance of this icon was immediately thought to be connected with that event. What is more, the priest was given to understand that the crown that had fallen from the head of the Tsar had been taken up by the Theotokos, the Mother of God: henceforth she would be the reigning Tsarina of the Russian state. Thus, the icon was named the "Reigning" icon and became widely revered among the Russian people.[31]

Wow, if that story is not enough to take your breath away! I am not surprised that the icon that was miraculously revealed had the Mother of God, sitting as a Queen on a throne, crown upon her head, holding a scepter and an orb. It appeared for all to see from a hundred years of basement obscurity, exactly on the Tsar's abdication day. Let us not forget, it was common knowledge that Tsar Nicholas II and his entire family deeply loved and revered the Mother of our Lord. In such dark times of satanic tyranny this icon itself was discovered as dark and murky in appearance at first. Just as the dream foretold, the colors would change and become clear and bright with time. In fact, the Mother of God's robe renewed itself to a red by many accounts, as if it was soaked with blood. In just over a year from the discovery of the icon the Tsar and his entire family would be slaughtered, shedding innocent Russian Martyr blood.

My spiritual Father Nektarios told me to look at this icon with my spiritual eyes. He told me that through suffering and bloodshed and many tears Russia would be forgiven after repentance. The Most Holy Mother of God would preserve Russia through the prayers of Tsar-Martyr Nicholas II and his Martyr family. I cannot even write about that night in this book. It hurts my heart too much to think of it again. However, Father Nektarios always reminds me to focus on the *joy*. This family is so beautiful that the more you study their photos the more uplifted you feel. The joy is for us now because God has given us these beautiful Saints as our new friends — both my friends and yours. Father Nektarios says to look upon their martyrdom as the day of their birth into Paradise. I tell him I hope they all died quickly. Father says that their deaths are a sacrifice for the Russian people they loved and served to the end. Father points out that these Holy Royal Martyrs are no longer just for Russia. They fulfilled a sacred calling for the *whole world*. The early Christian author Tertullian once said, "The blood of the martyrs is the seed of the Church," and the Body of Christ is a continual witness to this reality.

Even Saint John Kronstadt, who had deep ties to the Imperial family, was granted a miraculous vision in 1901 foretelling of the future (1918) martyrdom of Tsar Nicholas II. After evening prayers he laid down to rest before an icon of the Mother of God. He heard a voice which turned out to be Saint Seraphim of Sarov. The voice instructed him to arise and follow the will of God. So he stood up and saw the Saint crossing himself. Then Saint Seraphim began to show Saint John Kronstadt many disturbing, frightful and prophetic images. One of them concerned the Tsar:

"I saw the Tsar sitting on a throne. His face was pale, but brave. He was reciting the Jesus Prayer. Suddenly he fell like a dead man. His crown fell. The wild beasts, dogs, and scorpions trampled on the anointed Sovereign. I was frightened and cried bitterly. The Starets (Saint Seraphim of Sarov) took me by my right shoulder. I saw a figure shrouded in white. It was Tsar Nicholas II. On his head was a wreath of green leaves, and his face was white and somewhat bloodied. He wore a gold cross around his neck and was quietly whispering a prayer. And then he said to me with tears, 'Pray for me, Father John. Tell all Orthodox Christians that I, the Tsar-martyr, died bravely for my faith in Christ and the Orthodox Church. Tell the Holy Fathers that they should serve a Panikhida (memorial service) for me, a sinner, but there will be no grave for me!' Soon everything became hidden in the fog. I cried bitterly praying for the Tsar-Martyr. My hands and feet trembled from fear."[32]

Everything connected with our Lord God — from icons to people — was confiscated and eventually destroyed by the Russian revolutionaries who were under the influence of satan.

The Royal Family during their devastating imprisonment on their tragic journey to their eventual martyrdom.

I can understand Saint John Kronstadt's bitter tears. I, too, felt like crying when I first read his vision. I am only sharing a portion of it; it's too much to bear. I find it interesting how Tsar Nicholas II was revealed in this vision saying the Jesus Prayer. It's a prayer we are all encouraged to say repeatedly. He was human, of course, and a sinner like all the rest of us. However, we cannot forget that he was anointed King or Tsar in the name of the Holy Trinity, so his murder was not only a sin before people but also before our Great Lord God. A hundred years later, I still have a hard time thinking of that night. Whenever I think of the demons lurking in the darkness waiting to kill that Christ-like family, it makes me sick. But I will say one more thing about that horrible night of July 4/17, 1918.

In the basement room of the Ipatiev House where the Tsar and his family were executed, four Kabbalistic symbols were found. The meaning of these symbols consists of everything you might imagine it would say: "Here, under the command of satanic forces, the Tsar was sacrificed for the State's destruction. Let the world know this."[33] Ok, we get it, satan. You think you won by killing the Tsar. But you can never win. God always wins. Period.

The Tsar-Martyr's popularity is only growing with time and people love him and his beautiful family. My love for them is just a drop in an endlessly expanding pool. The truth is coming out for all who have eyes to see and ears to hear. I want to learn from the example of our holy Saints to draw even closer to God. The Holy Royal Martyrs were sacrifices for God and no one else. Even now, in Paradise, they are actively building God's Kingdom here on earth! Blessed are those who are persecuted for righteousness sake, for theirs is the kingdom of heaven. I have news for you, satan: They made it to Paradise! You may set your powers of hell loose on Earth, but you can never conquer Holy Russia and the Orthodox Church you tried to destroy. We are now rejoicing because we have great intercessors in heaven — Tsar-Martyr Nicholas II and his Martyr family. These Saints continually pray for those who call upon them and love God. Truth cannot be contained or destroyed. It's a done deal. God has *already* won, and peace and joy are already taking over. Amen!

\+ + +

Church On The Blood: Called the Church on Blood in Honour of All Saints Resplendent in the Russian Land, this church stands in Ekaterinburg on the site of the Ipatiev House, where the last Tsar of Russia, Emperor Nicholas II, his family, and members of their household were martyred.

Chapter Nine

THE MIRACLES BEGIN

"Blessed are you when men revile you and persecute you and utter all kinds of evil against you falsely on My account."

Matthew 5:11 (KJV)

Many miracles have been attributed to members of the Holy Royal-Martyr family. Here, the author holds an icon of Tsarevitch-Martyr Aleksei, from whom she had requested intercessory prayers on her behalf only days before receiving this icon as an unexpected gift.

The Miracles Begin

"Blessed are you when men revile you and persecute you and utter all kinds of evil against you falsely on My account."

When Lenin seized power in Russia, he unleashed a movement of all-out hatred of God. Call it what you will — the Bolshevik Revolution or Communism — the theme of this movement was atheism, the turning away from God. Everything and everyone was brainwashed against the Holy Trinity. For the next seventy years, human blood held this movement together. First and foremost on Lenin's execution list were the Lord's beloved Tsar-Martyr and his beautiful family.

Lenin did not know there is only one true God: The Holy Trinity, the one-in-essence true God. Communism exhibited its worst, most horrific persecutions against Holy Russia where God had been established as head. This revolution was not just a change of regimes. It was a spiritual war.

There is no doubt that the Tsar-Martyr and his Martyr family were and are spiritual beacons for the Russian Orthodox people. But what many don't realize is that the Tsar-Martyr should be loved and significant to *all Orthodox Christian believers.* As a pious Orthodox Tsar, we can understand the truth of how he restrained the appearance of the Antichrist — he got down on his knees before God and prayed for his country. Now, as a Saint, he continues to do so by building God's Kingdom here on earth. Myrrh-streaming icons and Holy Royal Martyr miracles continue to occur to this day. On more than one occasion, I have gotten into heated discussions with Orthodox believers who do not share my sentiments regarding the Tsar-Martyr.

On the other hand, many people like me agree Tsar-Martyr Nicholas II is one of the greatest Saints God has given us. Of course, He has given us many great Saints. How can one profess love for Saint Seraphim of Sarov or Saint John Kronstadt or Saint John Maximovitch and not be convinced of the Tsar-Martyr's greatness as a Saint? All of the aforementioned Saints openly acknowledged this Tsar's holiness. I think that anti-Tsar propaganda is still influencing people's opinions about Tsar-Martyr Nicholas II. It is a great spiritual loss for a person not to be aware of his spiritual legacy. I sincerely pray every believer embraces the sanctity of each member of this Imperial Saint family.

I am proud to say, as a Serbian-American, that the question of his glorification — which was a long time in coming — was first raised, not by Russians, but by my people, the Serbs. On March 30, 1930 a newspaper in Leskovac, Serbia (where my mother, grandmother, and great-grandmother used to live) published an interesting article. It was a telegram that stated an official appeal to the Synod of the Serbian Orthodox Church to go ahead and present the question of the glorification of the late Russian Emperor Nicholas II. Even today, I feel my Serbian friends also love the Russian people with all their hearts. We Serbs very much love, respect, and venerate Tsar-Martyr Nicholas II and his family of Holy Royal Martyrs.

I know this sentiment may not be shared by some younger Serbs, but those of us born before 1965 generally feel this way. We agree that he is a great Orthodox Christian Saint and was a devoted friend of the Serbian people. Furthermore, we perceive him to have been a most humane and pure-hearted ruler who died with the glory of a martyr's death. I pray the Serbs and all Orthodox Christians never lose their love for the great Tsar-Martyr Nicholas II. Hopefully believers who do not know the Tsar-Martyr in their prayer life will begin to feel compelled to call upon him too!

Holy Royal Martyr miracle reports started circulating not long after their martyrdom. The miracles which follow all came from the website set up by Archimandrite Nektarios Serfes. There you can read more about the Royal Romanov miracles, at http://www.serfes.org/royal.

One 1925 example was an elderly Serbian lady who had lost two sons in World War I, and whose third son had disappeared without a trace and was thought to be killed. After this devout mother finished her prayers for all those killed in the war she fell fast asleep. As she slept she dreamt of Tsar-Martyr Nicholas II. He told her that her son was alive and in Russia, where her had fought together with his two brothers. Then he proceeded to tell her that she would not die until she had seen her son. Soon after this dream she found out this message was indeed true! Months later, he returned from Russia and she embraced him with great motherly joy.

There followed more Serbian reports of Tsar-Martyr Nicholas miracles. In August of 1927, a Belgrade newspaper printed one that centered on a Russian Painter named S.F. Kolesnikoff, whose work I viewed hanging on the walls my childhood family home; later my Serbian-born mother Danica gave me a couple of his original oil paintings.

This is how the story goes. The artist was invited to paint the new church in the ancient Serbian Monastery of Saint Naum, which stands on Lake Ochrid. The painter was given complete freedom to create the frescoes adorning the inner dome and walls. While executing this project, the painter decided to paint the faces of fifteen Saints, placed in ovals, on the walls of the church. Fourteen of those Saints were done quickly, while the fifteenth oval remained empty for a long time, an inexplicable inner feeling impelling Kolesnikoff to wait. One evening Kolesnikoff came into the church during twilight hours. It was dark below and only the dome was lit by the sharp-edged rays of the setting sun. Evening in the church seemed mystical and unearthly. At that moment the artist saw that the empty oval came alive, and that from it looked down the sorrowful face of Emperor Nicholas II. Struck by the miraculous vision of the martyred Russian sovereign, the artist stood for some time as if rooted to the spot, feeling benumbed. Then, as he himself describes, feeling a rush of prayer well up in him, he leaned a ladder against the oval and without marking with charcoal the outline of the wondrous face, with brushes alone he outlined it. He could not sleep the whole night, and as soon as the first rays of sun appeared, he was already in church, sitting high on the ladder and working with such fervor as he had never known. As he himself writes: "I painted without a photograph. I had previously seen the late Emperor on several occasions and his face became indelibly etched in my memory. Now I finished my work and placed an inscription on this icon-portrait: '*The Russian Emperor, Nicholas II, who received the crown of martyrdom for the freedom and the happiness of the Slavs.*'"

What really touches me is a witness to this documented miracle:

Soon afterwards General Rostich, commander-in-chief of the Bitol military district, visited the monastery. Coming into the church, he looked for a long time at the face of the late Emperor painted by Kolesnikoff, and tears ran down his cheeks. Then, turning towards the painter, he softly said: "*For us, Serbs, this will be one of the greatest and most worshipped of all Saints.*"[34]

The author's favorite miracle concerning the Tsar: The arrow points to the oval which remained empty until the artist, Kolesnikoff, saw the empty oval come alive with the image of Emperor Nicholas II. This miracle occurred nine years after the Martyrs' execution in 1918 but before their glorification by the Moscow Patriarchate in 2000, at the ancient Serbian Orthodox monastery of Saint Naum. The monastery stands on Lake Ochrid. During his lifetime, the Tsar gave Kolesnikoff (one of the Tsar-Martyr's favorite artists) an engraved cigarette case.

Well, there you go, truer words were never said. As the daughter of Serbian-born parents, I dutifully continue this great love and respect for the Tsar-Martyr Nicholas II. I cannot help it. This is part of my roots and part of who I am. He is a great inspiration for me and hopefully my future generations. I can only hope this "labor of love book," inspires others to also love him and his family, and to *do good deeds in his honor*. This way we can pay back a debt of love we all owe him because Saints like the Tsar-Martyr take us by the hand and lead us to Christ. He was a Tsar who lived his life knowing that his Imperial Russian Crown was first and foremost a service to God. In turn, he inspires us to remember that our lives are also to be lived in service to God. The Tsar always stood firm in his faith until the very end.

+ + +

As I am writing this book we are living out the hundredth year of the Martyrdom of Tsar Nicholas II and his family *this very year*: 1918-2018. The year 2018 was a big deal in their remembrance, not just in Russia, but around the world. Their popularity took many by surprise. Those of us who already loved these Saints feel even closer to them, and many others were introduced to them for the very first time. There was a worldwide public outpouring of extraordinary spiritual love and respect for them. There was even a feeling of sadness and repentance that the Russian people, and even the whole world allowed these murders.

The revelation of the Martyrs' greatness was obvious to all who observed the hundredth anniversary. My friends who went to Russia were deeply moved by the processions, icons, and church services shared by all. You could see how many people were coming out of the woodwork saying: "We love these Saints!" When you stop and think of how the Communists tried to systematically erase their legacy forever, you see the heavenly triumph reveal itself. You cannot erase the truth. This family stood for the truth: The *Holy Trinity*. In fact, flash forward 100 years and icons of Tsar Nicholas and his family can be found in almost every church in Russia. Outside of Russia they are also loved. Here I am in Nashville, Tennessee with eight icons of these Saints in my home — and that doesn't even include my paintings of them! The communists did all they could to obliterate their memory — especially seeing how they were becoming a spiritual beacon amongst underground believers.

The decision was made to whitewash the place they lived and died in at the end, so the house they were murdered in was destroyed in an attempt to further erase their memory. Ipatiev house was demolished in 1977 for the sixtieth anniversary of the Russian revolution by orders of the Communist Party of the Soviet Union. It was another epic failure — another joke on satan. Thanks for clearing the ground for the magnificent church honoring them and for making room for the Holy testimony commemorating their lives. It's crystal clear that every target the Bolsheviks shoot for, meets with epic failure.

It is no surprise to me that the Holy Royal Martyrs have now become the most widely venerated Saints in Russia. We already know that they are continuing to gain popularity even beyond Russia. In another 100 years, these Saints will be loved even more. They have become part of the everyday spiritual lives of believers. For example, I was having a rough morning today and I stopped in front of their icon, crossed myself and told them my problems and asked them to pray for me. When my beloved dog MacDuff was dying of cancer, I asked Aleksei to pray for me to have God-given strength. I picked him because I knew he loved dogs. Skeptics may disagree, but I know he responded to my prayer. Two days after MacDuff died, I received a gift of an icon of Tsarevitch-Martyr Aleksei, pictured alone holding an icon of Christ. I had never seen him solo in an icon before!

The reports I hear and read of miracles and myrrh-streaming icons and photos of these Holy Royal Martyrs just keep coming to light. There is one that really hits my heart. Before the Ipatiev House was demolished in 1977, it served varied purposes. One of them was home to the Anti-Religious Museum. There is a miraculous story told to Archbishop Melchizedek, who had been |the Hierarch of Ekaterinburg for many years.

In 1990, an elderly woman came to his office to tell of her experience as a night guard for decades at the Museum in the Ipatiev House. The miracle she reported occurred in the same cellar room in which

Tsar-Martyr Nicholas and his Holy Royal Martyr family were led to slaughter like innocent lambs for the sacrifice and sins of their Russian people. In that cellar room they were all executed by Lenin's cronies early in the hours of July 17, 1918. The old lady told the Archbishop that the wall riddled with holes from the bullets of the regicides oozed blood for many years. The authorities would come and plaster up and paint over the wall, but drops of fresh blood continued to appear through the holes made by the bullets. She also said that on the eve of feasts, such as the Nativity of Christ, Pascha, and Pentecost, she heard beautiful singing. She was a night guard there, so she thought that the voices she heard sounded like angelic chanting or even heavenly hymns coming from the cellar. *Lord have Mercy, the Saints are alive.*

The Romanov dynasty was founded in the Ipatiev Monastery in Kostroma in the year 1613, and the dynasty fell when the Royal Martyrs were executed in this house by the same name: the Ipatiev House in Ekaterinburg, in July of 1918.

The bullet-ridden cellar in which the Holy Royal Martyrs and their personal attendants, who were also later recognized as Saints, were slaughtered. Even their family's pets were included in the wicked attack.

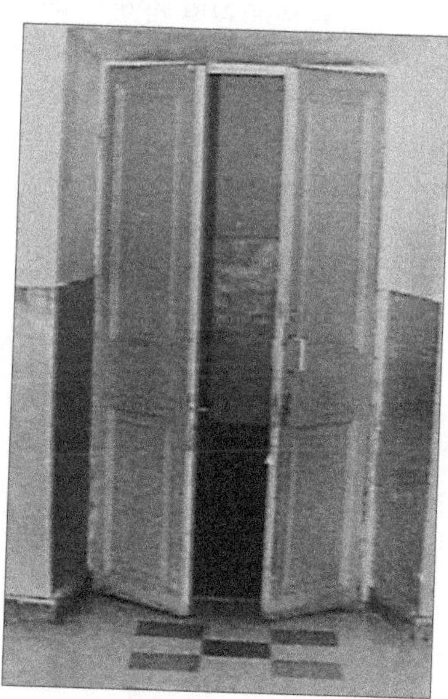

The doors leading towards the cellar where the Holy Royal family was executed. The Holy Royal Martyrs not only met their deaths after passing through these doors, but also their births into life everlasting in the heavenly Kingdom of God.

The Tsar and his family were moved to the Ipatiev House in April of 1918. Many people forget that they spent three horrible months of psychological torture there before their deaths. The only saving grace and miracle for them is that God allowed the family to all die together. Thank God for that! With every single photograph I have ever seen of them, I am absolutely convinced that they adored each other. Their example of Christian marriage and family life is another legacy of love they leave behind for us. I believe there will come a time when the majority of Orthodox Christian families will have an icon of them in their homes. They inspire us as a beautiful family inside and out. The Holy Royal Martyrs represent the quintessential Orthodox Christian ideal of a harmonious and God-loving family. They are our Saintly family role model in a day and age when the concept of Christian family life is becoming unclear and confused. These Saints can guide us, give us hope, and remind us to stick with Christian values in both good and bad times. They inspire us to stay together and show us how to keep God at the head of each of our families. When we do this faithfully — as they did — we sanctify ourselves and our blessed family life. I do believe getting to know these Saints individually and as a family is a gift available for all! It is time for *you* to have an icon of the Holy Royal Martyrs in your home.

\+ + +

Chapter Ten

FOLLOW THE HOLY ROYAL MARTYRS' FOOTSTEPS

"Rejoice and be exceedingly glad, for your reward is great in heaven."
Matthew 5 :12 (KJV)

Finished portraits of the Holy Royal Martyrs by artist and author Ariane Trifunovic Montemuro.

Follow the Holy Royal Martyrs' Footsteps

"Rejoice and be exceedingly glad,
for your reward is great in heaven."

An icon of the Great Tsar-Martyr Nicholas II and his consort Tsarina-Martyr Alexandra, and their children Grand Duchess-Martyrs Olga, Tatiana, Maria, and Anastasia, and Tsarevitch-Martyr Aleksei in your home, will visually remind you of these Saints who are now in heaven. They are your new friends. They have gone before you and me and they deserve our honor and praise. Our faith teaches us to commune with them; they hear us in heaven. These Saints can help us through their prayers. I know this is true because they continue to help me. They console us in our suffering and they continue to lead us to Christ. We must lift them up in our hearts and make them part of our lives. They will not only pray for us but also provide us with examples of piety, meekness, faith, and humility to live by.

The Most Holy Mother of God once instructed a young monk to go to the Island of Zalit to find and follow a man of great spiritual strength: Elder Nikolai Guryanov. She told the monk that this Elder is particularly dear to the Lord because he is one of the last pure souls. In him, all of you can see the precious manifestations of the Orthodox Christian faith and the highest love of Christ, which is rare and uncommon. Furthermore, the Elder Nikolai loves Christ and his neighbor so excessively that nothing could distract him from the love of God. That place on the island is to be sacred, because a Temple of the Throne of God will be erected there. So this is what the Theotokos told a monk who was seeking a mortal example of Godliness.

It gets better. Some of the icons that graced the walls of this blessed Elder's room were icons of The Tsar-Martyr Nicholas and his family of Holy Royal Martyrs! He kept photo albums, paintings and films of these Holy Saints in his room. Throughout his life, he honored and venerated them with admiration and devotion. It is obvious that he knew they were Saints way before they were canonized. At the end of his long life, he said, "I was ready long ago, it is a sin to remain here, my relatives are waiting for me: The Tsar and the Empress, Father John of Kronstadt, Illarion Gdovski, and my mom is waiting." The Elder also said one more thing before he died that gives us a clue as to how the Saints pray for us. "I will fly away on wings, I have huge strong ones and I will reach 'there' in that moment…and at Home will pray for you all." I love how he calls heaven home.

If we commune with Saints, like the Holy Royal Martyrs, maybe we, too, can have *huge strong wings* that take *us* home to heaven. Let us learn from them and follow in their footsteps. How I would love to have these strong Saints in my corner, rooting for my salvation!

Elder Nikolai Guryanov (1909-2002) loved Tsar-Martyr Nicholas II and his family so much he had icons and movies of them and he prayed that they would escort him to meet God when he died. You can see one of his icons of the Holy Royal Family on the wall behind him.

I have no doubt that Elder Nikolai Guryanov will also become a Saint one day. Christ was the center of his life. On his wall you could see the testimony of all the Saints he loved and revered.

Upon his deathbed, the Elder saw Holy Archangel Gabriel enter his room with a bouquet of lilies to symbolize the Elder's purity and holiness. When the Elder saw this he said, "He has blessed me, and crossed me with this lily!" The Elder then passed away on April 4th, 2002. After vesting his body the priest walked over to the Elder's coffin to place a blessing cross and Gospel book in his hands. When he was about to put the cross in the right hand, the Elder suddenly moved and took the cross himself in his right hand. The priest then leaned over and saw his left hand open to take the Gospel book. Miracles keep coming. So just from this, we already know Elder Nikolai is a Saint "in the works." I guess you can see one Saint leads to another.

As I said earlier, "like attracts like." The Saints are all connected to each other by God. They recognize each other. They are there for us. Even in our sinful state, they recognize our holiness. Many holy people and Saints already commune with the Holy Royal Martyrs. The Saints know we all have the potential to become like them. We must follow their lead and strive to know and imitate Christ.

Life is a precious gift. Our Saints' lives, in particular, are holy gifts from God given to each of us for our spiritual benefit. We just have to look and see. We have to choose either opening our spiritual eyes or listening to the propaganda of non-believers. I have noticed the older I get, the more spiritual beauty I perceive and discover in our Saints. I seem to see it more clearly the closer I get to my heavenly home. I had no awareness of this as a young woman. My life was ahead of me. Death was not in my mindset. The future possibilities were endless. Everything centered on me: My thoughts, my dreams, and my wants. I surely am one of many with a life-long list of sins — so many times I have forgotten to include God in my life. But the few times I did things right always involved me not making my own decisions. Things always turned out right when I involved God and His word in my decision. Even today, I do try harder, but honestly still struggle with trying to remember God in all things. That's where these Saints come in. They can help us feel less alone and always remember God by their life example.

In this very day and age, we are already marching into a more and more Godless future. A new generation of demonic cronies is currently lurking in the shadows of this Godless world. Are you ready? Gird yourself with the spiritual armor of the Saints and strengthen your future generations. Unless we prepare, history will no doubt repeat itself. The Holy Royal Martyrs gave us some sanctified footprints to follow. Let us follow them together! Learn the history of these Saints. Commune with them. They can literally save your soul.

Since Tsar Nicholas II was anointed by God in Church, this anointing cannot be removed by anyone other than the Tsar himself, who would have to renounce Orthodoxy. Tsar Nicholas, the great protector of Orthodoxy, remains Tsar forever — to all eternity. The tragedy is that the Russian people lose God's grace without their Tsar. Saint John Kronstadt said that Russia would be like a "stinking corpse" without the Tsar. We know as individuals, that we are nothing and nobody without God. We are dead without Him. People have to respect and submit themselves to the Tsar because he submits himself to God. That's the holy chain of order. It's a pattern we all have to learn and follow in our lives. Tsar Nicholas followed this perfectly on his end. It's pretty simple. *God comes first.* Reject the Tsar, and you reject God. The Russian people had a lot to repent for, for rejecting their Tsar. And so do we all.

This holy chain of order is the chain of *life*. In order to have life we must follow this order. Without the Tsar, death took over in every sense of the word. Lenin's revolutionary order of a new Russian life was death. So let's choose life. Choose to put God first. Set the order each day in the smallest of ways. The smallest life detail can order the biggest. It's as simple as a morning prayer and evening prayer and a prayer before each meal. Just like the Holy Royal Martyrs, we can all start our order right each day. A simple daily rule may even save our souls.

The actual coronation said it all. Vladyka (Bishop) Anthony Khrapovitsky loved to recall the Tsar's prostration before God and the Church which he makes during the coronation, while the entire Church, all its members, stand. And then, in response to his submission to Christ, all in the Church make a full prostration to him.[35]

Life with God first is really just simple spiritual common sense. That's why we kiss the hand of a priest, not for the priest but for the office he represents. It's the holy order of life. We are the servants of God. We need to remember our place in the order.

The Tsar-Martyr's sister Grand Duchess Olga remained dedicated all her life to this holy order, which she learned as a child: God first, then the Tsar. I believe her Orthodox faith and its teachings were her sustenance. She died in a foreign land with no outer semblance of her Imperial heritage, but she could never hide her regal bearing, pride, and great love she had for her family. She acknowledged on many occasions her unwavering belief in this holy chain of order. Her father and her brother were both tsar's by the grace of God. What a royal lineage Olga had! She knew they were both anointed in Church and this anointing was by God.

Not long before I was born in 1963, Ian Vorres, the author of her memoirs, asked her if she prayed for her brother. Her thoughtful response came out simply and clearly. "*Not for him — but to him. He is a Martyr.*" Her response came many decades before her brother's glorification. But Olga already knew. She knew he did God's will and was executed for being Tsar. It was an easy answer for her. She knew the order of life. Her brother was a true Christian Tsar whose destiny made him a martyr. One thing we can count on is if we do not follow this holy order of life with God first, then history will repeat itself.

There is no doubt that the last Tsar of Russia and his beloved family are *Saints*. I hope my book has laid any doubts to rest. Let us move forward and recognize their sanctity and be inspired by their holy lives. These Saints may even prove to be our saving grace. In the words of Father Dimitry Dudko: "The Tsar is a Saint and, moreover, one of the greatest Saints. O' great Saint of Russia, Great-Martyr Nicholas, pray to God for us!" So, let us always remember this Tsar gave his life for Christ. We can all be inspired by the lives of the Great Tsar-Martyr and his family of Saints. Our lives are filled with so many choices. May we all choose to follow their lead, because if we do, their holy Imperial footsteps will always lead us to the one True God. My *Debt of Love* for the Holy Royal Martyrs and Passion-Bearers of Russia will go on forever in my heart. However, this is where my story ends and our mutual prayer begins.

+ + +

O' Lord, send us patience
During these dark, tumultuous days
To stand the people's persecution,
And the tortures of our executioners.

Give us strength, O' God so righteous
To forgive our neighbor's wickedness
And to greet the bloody, heavy cross
With your meekness.

In these days of mutinous unrest
When our enemies rob us,
Christ the Savior, help us
Bear insult and disgrace.

Lord of the world, God of the universe,
Bless us with prayer
And grant peace to the humble soul
In this unbearable and fearful hour.

At the threshold of the grave
Breathe a power that is beyond man
Into the lips of your slaves
To pray meekly for their enemies.
Amen

— TSARINA-MARTYR ALEXANDRA, 1918

This beautiful prayer was composed by Tsarina-Martyr Alexandra only a few months before Lenin ordered her execution.

Tropar-Dismissal Hymn of the Royal Martyrs.

First tone:

Most noble and sublime was your life and death, O' Sovereigns; wise Nicholas and blest Alexandra, we praise you, acclaiming your piety, meekness, faith, and humility, whereby ye attained to crowns of glory in Christ our God, with your five renowned and godly children of blest fame. Martyrs decked in purple, intercede for us.

On the previous page was the first of the author's two favorite prayers; this is the second.

Epilogue

"Sillies, he will be higher than all the Tsars."
— Holy Eldress Blessed Pasha of Sarov

Center: Holy Eldress Blessed Pasha of Sarov

Not too long ago I drove up from Nashville to visit the Serbian Orthodox Monastery in New Carlisle, Indiana, called "The Nativity of the Mother of God." While I was there, I picked up a book in their bookstore: "*The New Confessors of Russia*," by Archimandrite Damascene Orlovsky. It is about the new Russian martyrs, confessors, and heroes of the Truth of God. This volume in particular deals with those that came from the area of Nizhegorod Province. These spiritual warriors were all Godly defenders against the dark forces of the Communist era. I was taken aback when I encountered a great slave of God in this book, whose full name was the Blessed Prascovia Ivanovna. She was known as a Holy Eldress and she was commonly known as the *Blessed Pasha of Sarov.*

Not only did this blessed one prophesize the arrival of the future heir of Russia, Tsarevitch-Martyr Aleksei, but she also had a private audience with Tsar-Martyr Nicholas and Tsarina-Martyr Alexandra during the time of Saint Seraphim of Sarov's glorification in 1903. The Tsar loved meeting her and commented that he liked her treating him not like a Tsar but like a simple human being.

Before her death in 1915, the Holy Eldress kept bowing (making prostrations) before the Tsar's portrait. She was already too sick to do so by herself, so she had others help lift her up and set her down. People asked her, "Why do you pray to the Tsar?" and she answered them, "Sillies, He will be higher than all the Tsars." Then she continued, describing him as, "I don't know… a monastic Saint; I don't know… a martyr." Not long before she died, the blessed one took down her portrait of the Tsar and kissed his feet with the words, "My dear one is already near the end."[36]

I hope that now, over 100 years later, their pictures go back up on our walls. Let our homes and churches be filled with Holy icons of these Holy Royal Martyrs. It is time to venerate and show our love for them. By doing so, we can repay the world's debt for not knowing during their lifetimes — and even now — the true holiness of these God-bearing Saints. God graciously gave them to us to strengthen our own faith, as they now intercede before Christ on our behalf. Since their earthly martyrdom, these Holy Royal Passion-Bearers have been in Paradise *fully alive*, just waiting for us to commune with them! I invite you to begin with these words, a prayer to the Holy Royal Martyrs by Father Nektarios Serfes:

+ + +

Holy Royal Martyrs,
Tsar Nicholas II and Family
Pray unto God for us!

Glory be to God for all things!

+ + +

O' Merciful Loving God!

Forgive us for having sinned before Thee in the merciless slaughter during the night of Thy beloved family:

The Holy Royal Passion-bearers Nicholas and Alexandra,

And Holy innocents Olga, Tatiana, Maria, Anastasia, and Aleksei.

Renew in us, O' God, Thy love and forgiveness,

That we may all walk once again on the path to salvation.

Lift up Thy hands, O' God,

Against pride, against the things which we have wickedly done in thy sight.

Greet within Thy Kingdom on our behalf Thy beloved royal martyred family whom we love.

Ask them to intercede and to pray for us.

Judge us not, O' God the King of ages,

To Whom belongs all Glory, Honor, and Worship unto the ages of ages.

Amen.

— Archimandrite Nektarios Serfes

Beyond Russia

The Centenary, July 1918-2018

Remembering the Holy Royal Martyrs in Nashville, Tennessee.

This photo was taken just following the Divine Liturgy commemorating the 100 year anniversary of the martyrdom of the Holy Royal Passion-Bearers at St. Innocent Russian Orthodox Mission, Nashville. Ariane's portrait of Tsar-Martyr Nicholas II had just been blessed by (second from left) Fr. Christopher, a priest from Alaska, and (third from left) Deacon Fr. Andre (+Memory Eternal) from Russia. They are flanked by the author (left) and her son, Tony (right).

Remembering the Holy Royal Martyrs in Russia

Jonathan Jackson and Elisa Vultaggio Jackson and their children Caleb, Adora, and Titus, in Russia at the 100 year memorial of the Martyrdom of Tsar-Martyr Nicholas II and his family.

Afterword

BY
JONATHAN AND ELISA JACKSON

Holy Royal Martyrs, pray for us.

Jonathan Jackson and Elisa Vultaggio Jackson with their children, standing in front of The Church on The Blood during their pilgrimage to Ekaterinburg. This church was built on the grounds of the former Ipatiev House; a chapel now stands where the Imperial family was martyred.

Our Love for The Royal Martyrs

My family and I were baptized into the Orthodox Church in 2012 at Holy Virgin Mary Cathedral in Los Angeles. Our journey to Orthodoxy was deeply connected with our experiences in this predominantly Russian Parish. Our hearts were set ablaze with love for Russia through the stories of Saint Seraphim of Sarov as well as through many of the parishioners we got to know along the way. But it took time. It was not a quick or easy journey. A turning point was when our priest, Fr. John Strickland, presented a teaching over the course of many weeks for Inquirers, titled "Holy Russia." To be honest, our reaction when he first proposed this to us was, "Holy Russia? What does that mean?" Being raised in America, those two words are never used in the same sentence. But as soon as we began to encounter the history of the Russian people and experience the beauty of their faith, we were awestruck. My wife Elisa chose Saint Elizabeth the New Martyr (the sister of Tsarina Alexandra) as her Patron. It was a bit of a mystery as to why she was choosing this modern Russian Martyr, with all the Saints throughout the centuries to choose from. However, it didn't take long for us to realize how blessed we were that Saint Elizabeth is interceding for us.

It was our love for Holy Russia that compelled us to begin reading more about the last Tsar and his family. We were drawn to them for reasons that are impossible to articulate rationally. We just needed to get to know them and their story. Nothing could have prepared us for what was to come. As we read more about their lives and martyrdom our souls were riveted and filled with grace and love for them. Nicholas and Alexandra's love for each other is a true inspiration for any marriage. The beauty, humility, and simplicity of their lives is radiant. Their love for their children is an undeniable witness to the goodness of God. The way in which all of them embraced the cross they were given and never returned evil for evil is enough to bring one to tears. Imitating Christ's humility, the most powerful man in the world accepts ridicule, mocking, slander, and death. These are the ones of whom Christ said, "Blessed are the meek for they will inherit the earth." These young Passion-bearers are glorious examples for our children, both in the way they lived and in the way in which they faced death.

My family was blessed to make a pilgrimage to Russia in 2018. It was a life-changing experience for all of us. There were so many moments that we will cherish for the rest of our lives, but there was one in particular that was the pinnacle. It was our time in Ekaterinburg at The Church on The Blood. We happened to be there for the 100-year commemoration of the Martyrdom of the Royal Family. Over a hundred thousand people are said to have been in attendance for the Divine Liturgy and Procession which followed. To see Orthodoxy in Russia rising from the ashes before our very eyes was moving beyond description. To be even more specific, the most powerful moment for all of us was kneeling down in prayer in the very room where they were martyred. The room or chapel is located underneath the main temple of The Church on The Blood. The most beautiful mosaic of the Royal Family glistens on the wall behind a small altar. It's stunningly beautiful. But something even more powerful than mere aesthetic beauty was present. It was the weight of holiness and grace. Tears streamed down the faces of everyone who prayed there. The Royal Martyrs are interceding for us all before the throne of God. And though they lost their earthly crowns they have gained everlasting crowns of glory. They shine not only as a beacon for the Russian Orthodox people but for the whole world through their love, humility, sacrifice, and faith. We are so excited and grateful to God that Ariane Trifunovic Montemuro has written ***Debt of Love*** so that more of us in North America can experience the grace of the Royal Martyrs and share their story with generations to come.

Holy Royal Martyrs, pray for us.

— Jonathan and Elisa Jackson

Learn more about Orthodox Christian Saints
by visiting the above website.

Let's fight spiritual blindness one Saint at a time!

Testimonial

BY

FRANCENE SAMARAS FOSTER

ORTHODOX CHRISTIAN PODCAST CO-HOST

Holy Royal Martyrs, pray for us.

Serbian Bishop Longin is pictured here with podcast co-hosts Ariane Trifunovic Montemuro and Francene Samaras Foster, just after he blessed their new Orthodox Christian Saint podcast series, "The Saints and Us, True Friends Sharing the True Faith."

To listen to these podcasts on Orthodox Christian Saints,
log onto
www.fellowshipofsaintmatronatheblind.com.

About the Author and This Book

I first "met" Ariane Trifunovic Montemuro on YouTube when I was searching for Orthodox iconography, and stumbled on her video describing how she was inspired to paint Saint Elizabeth the New Martyr. I am confident that with the premiere of this, Ariane's second, most gorgeous book, ***Debt of Love***, the Saints she loves are smiling down on her! Throughout the pages, she opens the doors of the Imperial Russian Palace to reveal the truth of these humble and faithful servants of our Lord and Savior, Jesus Christ. It is my hope that as you journey through this book, you will be as enlightened and as stirred as I was by the Holy Royal Romanov Martyrs, endearing yourself to them and feeling inspired and spiritually nourished, as though you just unwrapped a gift of Faith that will stay with you long after you are finished.

— Francene Samaras Foster
Orthodox Christian Podcast Co-Host
www.fellowshipofsaintmatronatheblind.com

At www.fellowshipofsaintmatronatheblind.com, all are invited to listen to the podcasts on the Holy Royal Martyrs and other Orthodox Christian Saints. You can enrich your spiritual life by learning more about the lives of the Holy Royal Martyrs (podcasts #9, #10, #11, #12, and #16).

Acknowledgments

Holy Royal Martyrs, pray for us.

The author's parents (above), standing in front of their Serbian coat-of-arms, and the author with her husband and children (below), in front of a statue of Tsar-Martyr Nicholas II located in Belgrade, Serbia.

A Note of Thanks

With eternal love to my husband Tony and son Tony and daughter Ana, and to my parents Danica and Aleksandar.

Special thank you to Father Benedict of Holy Cross Monastery in Wayne, West Virginia, for the Holy Royal Martyrs Holy Oil and to Kathleen McCollum for delivering it; and for the book cover cross which came as a gift from Elisa Vultaggio Jackson all the way from The Church on Blood, Ekaterinburg, Russia. All three of you friends in Christ confirmed the strong calling I was feeling to write this book.

Thanks for your enduring friendship over the years to Father Nektarios Serfes, my patient designer Elaine Millen, my talented publisher Mary Catharine Nelson, my sister Jennie Atty Gelles, my twin Francene Samaras Foster, Tim Weeks, Mira Gacic-Spalatin, and Christine Benagh (+Memory Eternal).

Most of all, I thank you Tsar-Martyr Nicholas II of Russia for your example of unquestioning dedication to the will of God, and to your beloved wife and children — martyrs in their own rights — who show me everyday that it is only through love that we can ever even hope to conquer the evil in this fallen world. My debt of love to you, my eternal friends in Christ, will never be fully repaid. I will love you all forever.

— Ariane Trifunovic Montemuro
December 2018
Nashville, Tennessee

Christ is risen from the dead,
Trampling down death by death,
And upon those in the tombs,
Bestowing life!

— Paschal Troparion

+ + +

The Saints are Alive!

The Saints are living with God and shall be forever.

Glory be to God!

Olga studying her photo album.

+ + +

If these Saints touched your heart, please consider giving any amount you can to: Holy Trinity Seminary Jordanville, New York.

Pay back a "Debt of Love" and honor Tsar Martyr Nicholas II and his family of Saints.

The author's first book,
I Shall Remember Thy Holy Name from Generation to Generation (above)
is available from all major online booksellers,
including Amazon.com.

Endnotes

Holy Royal Martyrs, pray for us.

Page xxvii: http://nicholaskotar.com/2017/05/26/coronation-nicholas-ii-triumph-tragedy/.

[1] *Orthodox Word*, Vol. 2, No. 5 (11) November-December, 1966. Inside cover.

[2] "An Orthodox Christian Confronts the Religion of Muhammad." http://FacingIslam.blogspot.com/2014/07/monument-to-tsar-and-passion-bearer.html.

[3] Kniga, Golubinaia, "Poem about the book of the Mysteries." Quoted in *Silence* by Mikhail Nesterov. http://orthochristian.com/100728.html. n.d.

[4] https://en.wikipedia.org/wiki/Russian_Orthodox_Church. n.d.

[5] Alexander, Bishop (Mileant), ed., "Orthodox Russia," in Missionary Leaflet #EA20 (La Canado, CA: Holy Trinity Orthodox Mission, 2001). Nicholas_ii_e.doc, 01-01-2001. 33.

[6] Viroubova, Anna. *Memories of the Russian Court.* (CreateSpace Independent Publishing Platform, 2014). 4.

[7] Ibid., 10.

[8] "Tsar-Martyr Nicholas II." www.fatheralexander.org/booklets/english/nicholas. n.d.

[9] Vorres, Ian. *The Last Grand Duchess.* (Toronto, Ontario, Canada: Key Porter Books, Ltd., 1964, 1965, 2001), 55.

[10] Ibid., 62, 63.

[11] Ibid., 65.

[12] Ibid., 63.

[13] Viroubova, Anna. *Memories of the Russian Court.* (CreateSpace Independent Publishing Platform, 2014), 37-38.

[14] Ibid., 40.

[15] Ibid.,198.

[16] Vorres, Ian. *The Last Grand Duchess.* (Toronto, Ontario, Canada: Key Porter Books, Ltd., 1964, 1965, 2001), 130.

[17] Ibid., 136.

[18] Bardovskaya, I. Bott, "The Last Home of Russia's Last Tsar." (The State Museum, Stp. Exemplary Printing House, Tsarskoye Selo, 2000), 29.

[19] Ibid.

[20] Zachariah, R. Monk (Liebmann), "Tsar-Martyr Nicholas II." https://www.fatheralexander.org/booklets/english/nicholas_ii_e.htm. n.d. 6.

[21] *New Confessors of Russia.* (Platina, CA: St Herman of Alaska Brotherhood, 1998), 260.

[22] "St. Seraphim's Canonization and the Russian Royal Family at Sarov." *Road to Emmaus: A Journal of*

Orthodox Faith and Culture. 61.

[23] Alfrerieff, Eugene E., ed. "Letters of the Tsar's family from Captivity" (in Russian. (Jordanville, NY: Holy Trinity Monastery, 1974)

[24] Benagh, Christine. *An Englishman in the Court of the Tsar: The Spiritual Journey of Charles Sydney Gibbes.* (Ben Lomond, CA: Conciliar Press, 2000). 55.

[25] Sheniloff, Matushka Natalia. *Russia's Crown Jewels: The Royal Martyr Children.* http://orthochristian.com/62837.html. n.d. 4.

[26] Ibid., 7

[27] Moss, Vladimir, *Tsar-Martyr Nicholas II, Restorer of the Orthodox Autocracy.* http://www.orthodoxchristianbooks.com/articles/827/tsar-nicholas-ii-restorer-orthodox-autocracy/. n.d.

[28] Ibid., 6.

[29] Moss, Vladimir. *The Russian Revolution: A Spiritual History, Part 2: The Gates of Hell* (1917-1945). (Vladimir Moss, 2009), 13.

[30] Ibid.

[31] Yazykova, Irina. *Hidden and Triumphant: The Underground Struggle to Save Russian Iconography.* (Brewster, MA: Paraclete Press, 2010), 47-48.

[32] https://www.imdleo.gr/daf/files/english/St_John_Kron/st-john, vision.html. n.d.

[33] "Life and Martyrdom of the Russian Royal Family," published by *Orthodoxe Kypsele*, in Greek. http://www.serfes.org/royal/miracle4.htm, n.d.

[34] *Orthodox Word Magazine.* "Seraphim Rose." http://www.holy-transfiguration.org/library_en/royal-nik.html. n.d.

[35] Moss, Vladimir. *Tsar Nicholas II Restorer of the Orthodox Autocracy.* http://www.orthodoxchristianbooks.com/articles/827/tsar-nicholas-ii-restorer-rothodox-autocracy/. n.d.

[36] Damascene, Archimandrite (Orlovsky). *New Confessors of Russia.* (Platina, CA: St. Herman of Alaska Brotherhood, 1998), 262.

CPSIA information can be obtained
at www.ICGtesting.com
Printed in the USA
BVHW071927091019
560658BV00002B/296/P